A people for His name

Duane & Sue Kershner with Judi Tabler

ISBN 978-1-0980-5959-0 (paperback)
ISBN 978-1-0980-8512-4 (hardcover)
ISBN 978-1-0980-5960-6 (digital)

Christian Faith Publishing, Inc.
832 Park Avenue
Meadville, PA 16335
www.christianfaithpublishing.com

Printed in the United States of America

Endorsements

A People for His Name is the story of a modern-day apostle! It reads much like the Book of Acts, revealing secrets and strategies of the kingdom of darkness and the kingdom of light. These true stories paint an undeniable picture of what it takes to advance God's kingdom in the darkest places on earth. We see how sustained faith and faithfulness is what creates the opportunity for miracles and environment for a great harvest of souls. After thirty years of personal relationship with Duane and Sue, I'm excited for this story to now be written down for the world to read. They are "heroes of the faith," and I pray this story will inspire many of us to serve the Lord in even greater ways!

—Reverend James Olson, President and
Cofounder, Catalyst Missions Group

An incredible story about two people "surrendering all" to the Lord, and then through relentless faith and *trust* were able to witness his blessings, glory, and plan unfold over decades. It illustrates how all the questions and concerns in the present that we ask God (Why are you telling me to do this or go there or give up that?) were answered in retrospection years later when you see how the beautiful mosaic of "divine alignment for a divine assignment" came together. How difficult it is for us to "wait upon the Lord," but when we do, he usually delivers more than we ask and greater than we can imagine. I was the typical "benchwarmer" Christian in the US Church. I went to Roca Blanca with a community group in 2010. Seven years later, I was diagnosed with an incurable disease. I had not spoken with Duane since 2012, and he was unaware of my illness. But as I was praying one morning for the Lord to allow me to "finish well," I received an e-mail from him that he had received a word from the Lord to contact me and tell me to come to Roca Blanca. He then briefly described a new healing ministry he had just started. I went and was healed in the Fountain of Grace, but more importantly, God revealed his plan for me to serve his kingdom for the time he had given back to me—to finish well. He has shown me signs and wonders—healings, deliverance, and even prophecies for me and my family, many which have already been fulfilled—all the things Christ said we could do in faith to further his kingdom work. Persecution of Christians and the Church has now reached the United States. Will you stand up, stand with, stand for, and stand firm for Christ? Or deny him to get along and not risk your job, friends, etc.? Your choice has eternal consequences. The Kershners' story illustrates what will be required of us going forward. I urge you to visit Roca Blanca to feel his presence, learn how to truly worship him, and to see signs and wonders that prove God is real and all powerful. Don't fall eighteen inches short of heaven because you know about Christ in your mind but don't really have faith and trust in him in your heart.

—David Blackwell, Retired Executive, Currently His Kingdom Servant, *Seeking Divine Alignments for Divine Assignments*

This book is filled with modern-day faith adventures with supernatural signs and wonders. Duane and Sue Kershner have demonstrated what it looks like to be led by the Holy Spirit, to be moved with compassion, and to not be afraid to believe God for His supernatural operations in and through their lives. As I read their testimony, I was inspired again about their faith, their commitment, and their obedience to God for these past fifty years. They have encountered the satanic realm and proven God's power is greater. In this book, they share how God has shown them how to respond in various situations, including some that were very challenging and dangerous. Anyone planning to go into missions would benefit from reading this book. They have learned how to believe for provisions, protection, and deliverance. They continue today moving in the Holy Spirit, training students, planting churches, and changing lives of people in Mexico, fulfilling Jesus's Great Commission. I have been to Roca Blanca mission base several times and have witnessed the amazing miracles of their lives and all those who they have reached. We are honored as a church to have been connected with them for over thirty years.

—Pastor Sharon Daugherty, victory.com, Tulsa, Oklahoma

Ruth Rohrer (Sue's mother)
Elmer & Ruth have visited Roca Blanca 7 times. This book is truly the work of God as recorded by Deanne.

This is now May 2021 and I give all the glory to God for the gift of the Holy Spirit.

Contents

Prologue

A people for his name will be redeemed by the blood of Jesus, "[o]ut of every tribe and tongue and people and nation" (Revelation 5:9). Beginning in the book of Acts chapter two, on that great day of Pentecost, with the Jewish people and then moving on to the gentiles in Acts chapter 10, the process of redemption has not stopped. However, in every case, someone must "go" to take out a people for his name.

In 1990, the State of Oaxaca in southern Mexico was classified as having the greatest concentration of unreached people groups in the western hemisphere: sixteen tribes of indigenous people, speaking 155 dialects, hidden away in the rugged Sierra Mountains. Who would go to take out this people for his name?

This book is the fascinating story of a young man, Duane Kershner, who was drafted into the army and sent to Vietnam. After returning from the war, disillusioned and in post-traumatic shock, he could no longer continue his architectural studies. In his desperate search for truth and meaning in life, he left the United States and headed for South America with no specific direction, only searching for truth.

After living with Zapotec Indians on an isolated beach in southern Mexico, a change occurred. Duane enrolled at a university in Mexico City. There he was ensnared by Satanists who were recruiting workers for The New World Order. Duane escaped from the Satanists in Mexico City but was cursed by them and brought to the point of death. He was miraculously brought back by the blood and power of the Lord Jesus Christ.

This is an amazing testimony of his conversion to Christ and his call to the indigenous tribes of Southern Mexico, to "take out a people for his name." Founders of the Roca Blanca Missions Base, Duane and his wife, Sue, have lived and worked with the indigenous tribes of southern Mexico for the past thirty years.

Part One:
Vietnam and the
Search Begins

1
The Beginning

And this is how it all began.

It was September of 1967, about two o'clock in the morning. I looked out from a window seat on a chartered commercial jetliner. The airline stewardess had kindly bid us "goodbye and good luck" as the crew disembarked in Manila. But the nervous joking and laughter soon subsided as we neared our destination, and the lights of Saigon were coming into view.

The silence was deafening. No one said a word. Silence. We couldn't speak what we were thinking because it was obvious that we were descending into a type of hell. The realization that some of us would never live through this experience filled our thoughts. Nausea filled my entire being as I began to distinguish the lights of Saigon from the many flashes of the war. Explosions in the distance were lighting up the darkness, while military flares and red streams of tracer bullets were pouring down into the blackness from helicopter gunships. It was a visual that I would witness a thousand times. *I still can't believe any of it. It's not real. It can't be.* These thoughts raced through my mind as the jetliner slowly descended.

I was now Private Duane Kershner, a member of the 189th Signal Battalion, fully dressed in combat gear including my M16 rifle that would stay with me day and night. All of this had happened so quickly.

It had been in my third year of architectural studies at the University of California, Pomona, when I received the dreaded letter from the US government. At the time, I had a good job and was doing well at school. It was 1967, and the Vietnam War was at its peak. I trembled as I fumbled to get the envelope open. I had been drafted and was given thirty days to set my affairs in order, report for my physical, and be inducted into the US army.

Oh no, this can't be happening to me! I groaned inside. *What? This is impossible!* Try as I may, I couldn't seem to wrap my mind around this shock. In haste, I made some plans, and a few days after receiving the notice, I dropped out of school, quit my job, sold my new Ford Mustang that I had bought with cash, and took off with a friend for Acapulco. I needed time to recalibrate.

After a week of drinking and considering if I should run or report, I reluctantly returned to Los Angeles and showed up for my physical exam. Having passed my physical, I then stood in a long line. I was going through the motions—they shaved off my hair, took away my clothes, outfitted me in army issue, and put me on a bus. This experience ricocheted in my mind like a fictitious horror movie. It was all too real. I was headed for Fort Ord, California, where for six months I learned how to kill. Another three months followed with intensive training in radio communications at Fort Gordon, Georgia. Once deciding where I would fit, the army trained me in two areas: one with a radio backpack to provide communications for search and destroy missions, and second as a radio teletype operator with secret "A" clearance status.

Throughout the duration of that year in Vietnam, I lived and worked in mobile radio teletype rigs. We were positioned in strategic locations, often in remote areas, our task to provide communications. These communications kept us up-to-date on the movements of the Viet Cong and the North Vietnamese army. The first four months in Vietnam, my assignment was to assist the 101st Cavalry Infantry Division. Later, during the January Vietnamese New Year offensive of 1968, I was transferred to a Marine unit about fifty miles south of the North Vietnamese border. We were shelled constantly day and night for eight months.

Finally, my time was up. For those of us who were drafted, our obligation was 365 days in Vietnam. Every soldier had a personal calendar, and each day that went by was another day checked off.

Another day alive. There were 58,000 of us that never checked off the last day. Finally, my day 365 arrived. My commanding officer released me to take a C-130 cargo plane to my point of departure from Vietnam! It was over! During that long flight to Seattle, Washington, where I would be honorably discharged, it seemed as though I was gradually waking up from a very bad dream. My mind was fogged from post-traumatic syndrome. Yet, I didn't really know that at the time. Nor did I know that my nerves had been badly burned from the effects of the chemical, Agent Orange, which had also left my face infected and scarred. I was alive physically, but aspects of my soul had died. Dreams I had once held were gone.

Within twenty-four hours after landing in Seattle, Washington, I was discharged from the US Army and released onto the street. I was on my own—dazed, confused, and in shock. My soul was in chaos. *Who am I? Where am I going? What do I do next?*

After checking into a hotel, I headed to a bar. But when I walked into the bar, there, in living color, the war was playing out on TV. Standing there alone, my heart began to race. I surveyed this crazy scene with my war-torn perspective. Was I on the same planet? People were oblivious—drinking, laughing, and having a good time. *Let me out of here!* I couldn't make sense of any of this. I turned an about-face and left. I began walking the streets aimlessly.

All my prewar ambitions were gone. Any once strong desires to complete my architectural studies had disappeared, and I no longer fit. I felt estranged from almost everyone. I was empty. What were my Kansas parents thinking? They had taught me that I should be "loyal to country," and now, I was extremely disillusioned. I had experienced, firsthand, something called, "The Military Industrial Complex."

My eyes had been opened. I had seen the mixture. Had it been purely a war for freedom, perhaps the suffering and dying would have been more meaningful. What about the thousands of innocent Vietnamese civilians who were wounded and dying? I was confused and wanted only to get away from it all.

2
My Search Begins

I made a brief visit to my family in Kansas. Feeling out of place and estranged, I left for Los Angeles to obtain my passport and get my visas in order. I was leaving for South America; no specific place, just leaving. During the process of the paperwork, I reconnected with former friends from my university days. Something had drastically changed. They were just the same, but who was I? The parties were the same, but I was on the outside looking in. I could not relate. Best friends from the former times got frustrated with me. I could not have fun with them. Finally, I said "goodbye" to the USA and headed south, not knowing where I was going and thinking possibly to never return.

I caught a train from the border town of Mexicali to Mazatlán, Mexico. After some days in Mazatlán, I hitched a ride on a petroleum ship. My job was painting the rails of the deck to pay my way. I was assigned to my own cabin and ate at the captain's table. Everything was looking better. Inwardly, something was happening to me. There was a strange awakening for *truth*. Was there a truth?

As a boy, my mother had taken me to church, but it seemed irrelevant and boring. In my backpack, I was carrying several paperback books I had selected. Was there an answer? I was growing desperate for answers. If there were none, it would be very difficult to simply live in a world that seemed so very lost.

Not knowing Spanish at the time when the captain of the ship let me come onboard, somehow, I understood that the tanker was going all the way to the Panama Canal. After three great days of

16

painting in the sunshine and looking out over the deep blue ocean, my captain friend pulled the big tanker into a port. Where were we? He then began to use his English and motion to me, saying, "Finish!" The ride was over! We were at a place called Salina Cruz, which is a port on the southern coast of Mexico.

Salina Cruz was the end of the line for the oil tankers and a very ugly place in those days. However, a few kilometers down the beach to the south was a cove, a virgin beach called La Ventosa. The inhabitants were families of fisherman, mostly of Zapotec Indian descent. Although we couldn't understand one another, they seemed to like me. I lived under a palm thatch on the beach, and in exchange for helping to pull in the fish net each evening, the natives happily gave me fish. I loved it there, and since I had in my backpack a series of books called *The World's Greatest Thinkers*, I had all I needed to find answers to my search. This wasn't so bad! *There has to be an answer*, I thought, as I poured over Plato and Aristotle.

Days passed and then, to my surprise and displeasure, a couple in a Volkswagen van with a New Jersey license plate arrived at "my" La Ventosa. I kept my distance, not wanting to be bothered. But my peace was not to be. One morning, the woman from the van searched me out in desperation. She was crying and beside herself, blubbering that her husband was a heroin addict. They were out of drugs, and he was experiencing withdrawals. Reluctantly, I approached the van. He was throwing up and doubled over on the floor of the van in a fetal position. The woman pleaded with me to help her drive the van to Mexico City to get drugs for her husband. One thousand curves of dirt roads over the Sierra Madre mountains and many hours later, I parked the van in downtown Mexico City. I said goodbye and walked away, never to see the couple again.

3
Tara

Mexico City was a big change from La Ventosa! However, should I really try to go back there? Were there really any answers? Somehow, I had heard about a bilingual university. It was located just outside of Mexico City on the super highway to Toluca. It was a well-known bilingual diplomat school specializing in international relations. I could attend under the GI bill which would pay for my education. I was troubled. The money I would receive for my studies seemed like "blood money" to me. But perhaps I could find another way to support myself.

Even though my search at La Ventosa had just begun, and South America was still in my heart, I decided to enroll at the University as an international relations major. Perhaps I could do something for peace and help this mixed up world somehow. After studying there for a year and a half, I was totally bored. The courses seemed empty and dry. Deep within, I was still crying out for "the answer."

I survived the congestion of Mexico City for one year with its traffic, smog, and noise, commuting daily to the university. Then, to my relief, I found a quiet apartment in a eucalyptus grove only a couple of kilometers from the university. Occasionally, I walked to school with my neighbor. Her name was Tara. She was from Pennsylvania, completing her last year of studies as a creative writing student. Eventually, we began to share meals together, and after a while, I moved in with her. For six months, we lived together. She loved me, so it seemed.

However, I still hadn't found my "truth." My studies at the university were mostly academic and provided no real answers. I was going through the motions, reserved and empty. I had no real understanding of Christianity, no belief in Jesus, and much less in Satan. Therefore, I was totally blind and deaf to the reality that Tara was a Satanist and that Satanism had invaded the university like a cancer. In fact, this university had secretly become, in certain aspects, one of the many training centers for those who would become future leaders in "The New World Order"—the final world government that will be led by the Antichrist.

Tara, in the most subtle and indirect ways, was working on me, endeavoring to get me open to her experiences, the "spirit world of demons" that she knew and in which she had learned to operate. Unbeknownst to me, her friends were Satanists too. They became our friends. One of her friends by the name of Grant would come to our apartment rather frequently to visit and share a meal with us. I was ignorant as to who he really was.

Tara and I had been together about three months when one evening, while relaxing together, I had my first "spiritual experience." I am sure Tara was very pleased about my "breakthrough." With no understanding of what was happening, my soul traveled out of my body. I experienced something called "astral projection." I was "outside" and in another dimension. I had no idea how long I was out there.

I clearly remember seeing a silver cord connecting my soul to my body, and it was as if I were floating around "out there" effortlessly. It resembled the pictures of astronauts floating outside of the space capsule but connected by life-support cables. Other beings were floating out there as well, ghostlike figures in appearance who communicated not by talking but simply by thought. They looked like vapor or smoke-like figures. Eventually, I was back in my body.

I was astonished! I was so weak afterwards that the following day, I stayed home from all my classes. Tara was inquisitive about "my experience." She of course knew that I had just experienced my first astral projection.

Those travels "out there" are to lead one to higher dimensions and into contact with spiritual beings which are really demonic principalities and powers. Once a person masters "travel," he or she can come back with information and instructions. A "skilled traveler" can even make visitations to people and places. To become an effective leader of a government that is to be ruled by fallen angels and the head fallen angel, being Lucifer, one is required to undergo training, to be in contact with the rulers of this present darkness.

> For we do not wrestle against flesh and blood,
> but against principalities, against powers, against
> the rulers of the darkness of this age, against spir-
> itual hosts of wickedness in the heavenly places.
> (Ephesians 6:12 NKJV)

I experienced this "travel phenomenon" twice within the next couple of months. The training was becoming more intense, and I felt increasingly ill at ease. At one point, I argued with Tara about what was going on, and we began to have some major difficulties in our relationship. Finally, I got the courage to tell her I was moving out. She cried, and in no way was she in agreement. However, I began to look for a place to live.

Strangely, a couple of days after my decision to move, a man at the university named Victor approached me. he seemed to know I was looking for a place. Victor told me that he and Mary (his live-in) had an extra room up the street from where they lived. He told me it was unoccupied, used only to store some of their things. I could have the room at no cost, he added. I rented the room and moved in. The room was in a large house in a mountain village a few miles up the mountain from the university. Little did I know that I was being set up. I would later find out that other Satanist friends lived in the same village and at the same boarding house. I was jumping from the frying pan and into the fire.

The village was located up the road from a national park; the mountain air and the pines offered a special attraction to me. Other students from the university also lived in the village. At times, we would ride to school together, and gradually, I was feeling familiar with the area. Mostly, however, I stayed to myself and avoided student parties, which were full of heavy drugs. I had seen enough of my share of drugs during the war. Instead, Tara's friend, Grant, would come to see me, and we would share a few beers.

4
The Spell

There was something strange about this guy, Grant. He was in his early forties, and it appeared that he had plenty of money. He was only enrolled in a few classes at the university but mostly, it seemed, he did nothing. Who was he?

Victor, who rented me the room, also gave me an uneasy feeling. He was in his late thirties and was studying international law. Supposedly, he was from Texas. If I did go to student parties, he was there. There was another man; I never knew his name, but if there was a party, he was there as well. I thought he might be a narc (narcotics officer). Once, I remember attending a party, and this nameless man was accompanied by a youth who was like a zombie. The youth had to be led about and cared for. His eyes seemed to cry out to me, and I felt very uncomfortable.

Mary, who lived with Victor, was in my Mexican history class. Sometimes we would study together. One Saturday, Mary invited me to her house to study for finals scheduled for the following Monday. After several hours of study and conversing into the late afternoon, Mary insisted that I stay for pizza. She related that Victor would be back and that other friends were coming.

Reluctantly, I stayed. Mary put together the pizzas and gradually, five or six others showed up. Mary had also prepared a flavored "Kool-Aid" type drink. As we sat around the table, eating, everyone seemed very quiet. The music playing was The Rolling Stones song "Sympathy for the Devil." Little did I know then that each one around the table was a Satanist. They had planned a Black Sabbath.

The purpose of this Black Sabbath satanic ritual was to bring another "recruit for Satan" and "cross the line" into the satanic workforce; unknowingly, I was the recruit! To become one of them required becoming demonized, receiving a demon or demons into your being.

To become a Christian requires receiving the Spirit of Christ into your being, being born again of the Spirit.

> God has sent forth the Spirit of his Son into your hearts. (Galatians 4:6)

We become children of God by receiving the Spirit of Christ in us. When an evangelistic altar is developed and the call made, people receive Christ by surrendering and accepting God's only Son, Jesus.

To become a Satanist requires receiving a demon spirit. They, however, do not speak plainly. Their method is by occult practices and the use of drugs; the "Kool-Aid" I was drinking had been drugged. The Satanist also used the power of music.

As we sat around the table, with the music playing (satanic music), drinking the Kool-Aid and eating the pizza, my Mexican history notebook was lying in front of me. Mary was sitting next to me on my right and was doing strange things. She held a metal writing pen in her hand and was drawing funny little figures on her notepad to the rhythm of the music.

Suddenly, I didn't feel well. Something was very wrong. I felt dizzy, and it seemed like the walls were moving. I looked around at everyone and realized that all eyes were on me. Mary placed the pen she was using on the table beside me, and I began to hear a voice saying, "Pick up the pen."

I was resisting. Something inside of me was saying, "No, don't do it." This battle continued while I was being intently watched by those around the table. Finally, I yielded and picked up the pen. It was hot. With the pen in hand, I began to automatically draw on the page in my history notebook that was in front of me. The drawing at the top of the page was of a dragon with a flood of water coming out of its mouth. On the bottom half of the page, my hand drew a very evil-looking mask. This strange phenomenon of the drawing happened supernaturally in seconds!

As soon as I finished the drawing, the music stopped. Some terrible dark power came into the room, the atmosphere changed, and the Satanists began doing something. Like the times my soul had left my body before, the same sensation was happening again; only this time, I was fighting to not let go. This unexplainable spiritual pull continued while someone read from what I now believe was the satanic bible. I could hear someone's voice speaking loudly words that seemed very powerful and mysterious. I began to lose strength and felt my soul slipping out. However, I kept fighting to not let it happen. This struggle continued for some time.

The speaking continued, but the "spell" was breaking, and they began to threaten me. They were frustrated that I was not yielding. Had I yielded, a demon spirit would have come into my being. As I have stated, the Black Sabbath is a copy of Christ coming into one's heart where the new birth of the spirit happens. This too requires a surrender. Now, somehow, I was not yielding, and the satanic process was dragging on.

An important thing I can remember is that one of them began to persuade me, coaxing me on and promising that if I took this step, I would become a member of "The New World Order!" They began to make serious threats, and finally, I bolted. Mysteriously, before busting out the door, I tore the page out of my notebook where I had drawn the dragon and the mask. Once out the door, I began climbing over the locked front gate of the property. Just as I was coming down on the other side of the gate, Victor came out of the house and nailed me. He was using some type of demonic mind control; his eyes locked onto mine, and I was frozen. He smiled and calmly began to unlock the gate, opening it as I climbed down. He began to tell me that I would never escape, that if I didn't give in, I would be found dead in the morning from an overdose. It would simply look like just another dead druggie, and no one would think differently.

He calmly came through the opened gate while maintaining me under his control. After more lies and threats, I suddenly broke away and began to run up the road to my house. I was certainly in better shape than he was. My army training was still with me.

As I approached my gate, Victor was not far behind. I got through the metal gate and slammed it shut. It locked! I was in the courtyard of my house with the gate shut, but then in the darkness, across the courtyard, I saw two figures going up the steps to my second-floor room. *Oh no! Who are they?* I banged on the door of the guy who lived below me. His name was Fleetwood. He opened his door as if he had been expecting me. He had! He was one of them! I stepped inside, explaining that someone was above us in my room. He encouraged me to sit down, then I looked at him and saw the same demonized eyes. Fleetwood began the same satanic persuasion all over again. Demonic power was coming through him by the words he spoke.

I broke away, busting out the door. I ran across the courtyard and up three flights of stairs to the rooftop of the house. The lady of the house did the laundry there. From the rooftop, I could see two men in the courtyard below. They stood for some time, watching me. There were numerous flowerpots on the roof, and I decided that if they started up the stairs, I would throw the pots at them. After what seemed like an eternity, the two went inside. By now, it must have been 4:00 a.m. The sky was totally clear, and the stars were so close that it seemed as if I could reach up and touch them. I wore only shorts, sandals, and a T-shirt. I was cold and shaking.

5
On the Run

The effects of the drug and the satanic spell were beginning to lessen, and my mind started clearing. I began to question what had happened. Did I have a mental breakdown? Was it even real? I had no understanding that I had just escaped from a Black Sabbath ritual. I had no knowledge of demonization, astral projection, Satanism, or the New World Order. I was a lost soul, a misplaced Vietnam veteran, alone on a rooftop in Mexico at four o'clock in the morning, cold, scared, and shaking.

There were terrible times during Vietnam, but I never cried out to God. My mother was a member of the Seventh Day Adventist Church. As a young boy, she had taken me along with her to the church services. Somehow, during all those years, I never heard about Jesus. It was mostly a religion about the Sabbath Day. My dad never mentioned anything about God to me.

As a teenager, I drifted away from any belief, and during my university studies, before the war, I lost all "God consciousness." I began to believe there was no God. My work, studies, and social life seemed to be all there was to life. During my time in Vietnam, I was shaken to the core but never cried out to a "higher power." Now, having left country and family, angry and confused, here I was on a rooftop in a mountain village in México.

As I stood there, shaking, had I lost my mind? Or did I just experience a life-threatening situation? I had heard real words, hadn't I? Didn't they say, "We will kill you"? It was all so unbelievable! I looked up at the stars and, out of the depths of my being, asked someone out there, "What just happened to me? Did I really just experience a life-threatening situation?"

To my surprise, a star fell! I asked again, "Was it real?" And another star shot across the clear sky! Someone was listening to me! Seven times I asked, and seven times, a shooting star shot across the sky in front of me! It was real! "What should I do?" I asked. In my mind's eye, I saw the face of a gentleman professor at the university. Inwardly, I knew that I should go to him. I hadn't had a mental breakdown; my life was in real danger.

Tara and I had been to the professor's house together for social events. He was an instructor in the creative writing department, an older Catholic gentleman who lived in Mexico City. I knew that I must find this man. I waited on the rooftop until the first 5:00 a.m. market bus came rattling down the mountain. As soon as I heard it, I got ready, and just as it was close enough, I ran down the steps, through the courtyard, out the gate, and jumped onto the bus. By late Sunday afternoon, I was at the house of the man I was looking for.

Because of his kindly manner, the professor invited me in. I was very emotional, and as we sat in his living room, I began to pour out my story. He listened very patiently and then quietly invited me to walk with him to a large Catholic church. No one was in the church, and my friendly helper sat me in a pew fairly close to the front. He then went to the altar, knelt, and prayed. When he finished, he took me back to his house and let me stay there for the night.

The next morning, very early, he and I were on the bus for the university. My thoughts were running in all directions. We were very quiet. Then, he gently took my hand and told me that I must get out of the country at once. He assured me that he would inform my instructors that because of an emergency, I had left for the United States. He comforted me, assuring me that I would not lose my credits at the school. He informed me that something truly was going on, that I could be killed. Several bodies had been found in the canyon below the university campus and again, he insisted that I must get out of the country. Even though he was very kind in his manner of speaking, I was in shock.

Our bus arrived at Chapultepec Park in Mexico City, and we both got off. He was going to catch the next bus to the university, but what was I to do? He placed a Virgin Mary medallion in my hand, held it tightly, and wished me well. Then he was gone! I never saw him again. I stood there on the street, wearing the same sandals, shorts, and T-shirt, with no ID, and very little money. My passport, Mexican visa, and all the money I had were at my room in the mountain village! I could not go there.

Grant lived in an expensive apartment close to Chapultepec park. He was my friend, or at least I thought so. I walked to his house and knocked. As he opened the door with a smile and greeted me, I noticed his eyes. They were the same eyes I had seen Saturday night! He said he had been expecting me! *Oh no! Him too?* Grant took me for a walk and said something about the time "it" had happened to him and how there was no way out. I was lost! No way out of what? And what was "it" that had happened to him? Grant never used words like Satan or the devil. As we walked, he spoke confusing words and mystical jargon. Suddenly, I turned and ran. Grant didn't follow. He knew better since there would be other opportunities and better ways.

I walked to Londres Street in the Zona Rosa of Mexico City where my friend, Carol, lived. Carol was Jewish, from New York City, and engaged to marry the governor of the state of Michoacan. *She couldn't be one of them*, I thought. Her brother attended the university, and somehow, I became acquainted with them. Carol was always friendly, and upon my arrival at her apartment, she welcomed me. I simply told her I needed a place to stay for a couple of days. She offered me a change of clothes as I remember. My stay at the apartment was no problem for her. She left, and I remained there alone.

During those quiet hours, I meditated on who were the "others" that could be part of whatever "it" was. I remembered the nameless man I had seen around the school who seemed to be doing something. But what? I recalled how the student body president had suddenly left the university with his family. The rumor was that someone was practicing witchcraft on him. The last time I saw him at school, I joked, "What's this witchcraft stuff?"

He looked terrified, did not say a word, and quickly walked on. I began to remember other similar situations.

Carol arrived home later that afternoon. About 7:00 p.m., there was a knock at the door, and a young woman who knew Carol arrived there with a man—the same man I had decided in the afternoon was one of them. The woman invited Carol and me to a party. I moved to the kitchen to get away, but the man soon followed me there. Carol continued talking to her friend in the other room. I recognized the eyes of this man, the same eyes I had seen the night of the "pizza party" and the same eyes that I had seen in Grant. The man opened up with, "I hear you have had a spiritual experience." His tone was not friendly. "You are going with us."

Carol, knowing nothing, was joyfully encouraging me to go. She had no idea what was happening. It was mind-control again, and I found myself walking down four flights of stairs with this man and woman I didn't know. My heart was pounding, but I couldn't do anything to get away.

We got into a car, me in the back, and for some time, we drove in the Mexico City traffic. After a while, we stopped in front of a large apartment building. The woman got out and called up to someone in the window of the second floor. The man driving told me brusquely to get out. We walked up the stairs of the apartment building and into a party. It wasn't just any party. It was the birthday of the son of the Secretary of the Interior of Mexico. We attended the same university; I knew of him. This was a high-class event with bartenders, people dancing, and members of the group Brazil 66 who were quietly playing. There were moviemakers from Canada and many others. Why was I here? The people who brought me disappeared into the crowd. The bartender brought me a drink.

A fellow from New York City who spoke only English began visiting with me. We were served another drink. My newfound English-speaking friend would occasionally dance with his wife, then continue talking to me. To this day, it is hard to understand why I did not try to get out of there. Instead, I began to let down and relax. It was a trap.

The fellow from New York began to get loud, and his wife took him into a back room. After some time, she came out very frightened and asked if I put something in his drink. I was astounded. Some moments later, he was carried out, yelling and out of his head. People started leaving. I was totally confused! A man I had never seen before came to me and sternly told me that this fellow from New York, who had been taken out screaming, had drank the drink intended for me. Then, very angrily, he told me the best thing I could do would be to commit suicide. I ran!

The following days in Mexico City were unbelievable. I was scared, confused, and running, but I was beginning to understand some things. On the subway, a popular song was playing by the group Santana, and the words were, "Got a black magic woman, she's got me running, hiding, uptown, downtown, she's trying to make a devil out of me."

The words opened up in my understanding. Yet, how could I get out of Mexico City? My passport and the funds I had were all in my room.

Then an amazing thing happened. Carol invited me to travel by train with her to Dallas. She had wanted to do this for a long time. She offered to pay for my ticket if I would go with her as a friend. She never knew what was happening with me, and I never told her. God used her to get me out of México City. I left my passport, Mexican visa, books, clothes, and all that I had in my room in the house where I had been living. I have never been back there. On the train, mysteriously, I was never asked for any papers! We arrived in Dallas, I thanked Carol, and never saw her again.

I looked up a high school friend in Dallas whom I hadn't seen in ten years. He was married, had two children, and welcomed me. Here I was in Dallas. Now what next? How could I tell anyone about this? I couldn't. Sometimes I would think, *Did it really happen?* Then I would remember the shooting stars and the professor who had helped me. It all seemed so unbelievable.

My friend owned an old second car that he loaned to me. To get out of the house, I would go to Grapevine Lake to walk and try to figure it out. Sometimes I would sleep in the car at Grapevine. My friend was fighting with his wife, and eventually, they divorced. To be at their house was a tense situation.

One Sunday afternoon, I returned from Grapevine, and my friend told me that I had a visitor from Mexico City, and his name was Grant! My heart began to pound! They found me! It was just like they said: "You will never get away." Grant had flown from México City and had come to the house where I was? This was incredible! How did he know where I was? He never came back, but I began to get mysterious calls at night. The voice would say, "We have candles burning for you and you will become ill and die. No doctor will be able to help you."

I began to work and soon moved away from my friend. I was alone, estranged from my family, and had no one. Who would believe my story? The oppression got worse. I was losing weight. My health deteriorated. Then my urine turned dark and there were pains in my right side. I was really frightened.

6
One Man's Obedience and the Greatest Miracle

Because of the faithful obedience of one man, I was given the way out.

I was browsing in a store when I met a man and his daughter. They were Spirit-filled Christians. The man, whose name was Charles McGee, began to speak with me. He and his daughter both saw that I needed help. Charles asked if we could talk, and I somewhat reluctantly agreed. He came to the place where I was living, and fearfully, I began to tell Charles the whole story. He boldly told me that "it" was satanism and that the Satanists would kill me. He explained the only way out was to call on the blood of Jesus.

Charles tried to pray with me, but I felt very much like I did on the night of the "Black Sabbath." I couldn't surrender. I got scared and I locked up. I didn't know if I could trust Charles. Who was he? He left and called the prayer chain of his church. He then returned and took me to a doctor. It did not take the doctor long to diagnose that I had advanced hepatitis.

Charles put me on a flight to Wichita, Kansas. My parents met me there, and this was the first time we had seen each other since I returned from the war. The small-town family doctor told my parents to take me home because there was nothing he could do. I had lost forty-five pounds, my hair was dead, and my skin was yellow. For three weeks, I lay in bed, getting weaker each day. Inwardly, I knew it was not just natural hepatitis. It was because of "them" that I was dying. This terrible illness that was affecting my body had come from the Satanists. They had cursed me to death; they had told me I would die and that no doctor could help. It was all so unbelievable yet real.

Then, one night around midnight, it was almost all over. I saw three dark "beings" come into the room where I was lying. The one in the middle was larger than the other two. I believe that one was the "Reaper." They waited at the foot of the bed. Death comes to separate the soul from the body, to cut the cord.

Please consider the following scripture.

> Remember him, before the *silver cord* is severed, and the golden bowl is broken; before the pitcher is shattered at the spring, and the wheel broken at the well. (Ecclesiastes 12:6; emphasis mine)

It is now my personal understanding that Death is a personality. It comes to "cut the cord," separating the soul from the body. Hell is not only a place but also a personality: Consider this scripture: "Then Death and hell were cast into the lake of fire" (Rev. 20:14).

It is my consideration that for those who have not been redeemed by the blood of Jesus Christ, at the time the body dies, a spirit comes from hell to escort the soul to its place in hell. There may also be a spirit that comes for the unredeemed body to accompany it to the grave. I only know this: there were three very dark beings that came into my room and waited at the foot of the bed where I had been lying for three weeks.

Around 4:00 a.m., Death began its work. A very cold feeling began to move up my legs, and it was as if every cell in my body opened up and the life was flowing out. The spirit of death continued to move up my body. I was saying no, trying to stop it. When it reached my chest area, my soul departed out of my body. However, this time, there was no attached silver cord like those times when I had gone out before, during astral projection. This time, I was free-falling in outer darkness into hell.

Seconds went by; then mysteriously, I could hear the words of Charles McGee, the man who had spoken to me three weeks before, trying to get me to "plead the blood of Jesus." This time I screamed out, "The Blood of Jesus!" That instant, *Jesus* caught me by the right arm of my soul. For a second, he literally embraced my soul, then he released me, and as he did, I stopped falling. A moment later, his blood flowed over my soul. *It was still warm!*

Instantly, I was back in my body, alive from the dead and under the blood. I gasped! The power of God, eternal life, resurrection power, filled every cell of my body. I was alive, and his healing power was exploding inside of me. The three demon personalities that came for me were gone. For the first hour, I cried and repeated his name, "Jesus, Jesus" over and over. How precious did that grace appear the hour I first believed. I understood. The search was over. It was December 17, 1970.

This was the answer; there *is* truth. I had not found it at La Ventosa. At the university in Mexico City, the devil had extended his hand. He had offered me a position in his New World Order, his "world government" that he will lead before Jesus Christ returns to completely destroy the works of the devil and take up his throne in Jerusalem. The devil's disciples had worked very hard. When they could not get me across the line and into full-time service, the next option was hell—the last option. The devil would have won had someone not spoken to me. I would be his captive today! Charles McGee has gone on to be with the Lord, but I will be eternally grateful for his boldness.

Now I was truly alive! The first day of life, I was gaining strength. I reached for my wallet. In it was the paper with the demonic figures I had drawn the night of the Black Sabbath pizza party. I had kept that paper for months, knowing that these symbols meant something. I took the paper out and asked my Father God, "What are these two drawings, the dragon and this ugly mask?"

I heard his voice for the first time ever. He said, "Turn the page over. The answer is on the back!"

I turned the page over, and there in my Mexican history notes, I had written two entries, "The Economic System" at the top of the page and "The Church" halfway down the page. I had never finished the outline. I looked again at the drawings. The dragon at the top of the page on one side and at the top on the other side were the words,

"The Economic System!" This was supposed to apply to my Mexican history class.

I looked at the mask again. As I meditated, I turned the page over, and there were the words "The Church!" These words were aligned at the same point on the opposite side of the page. *Oh! I get it! The two main strongholds or seats of Satan are the economic systems and the man-made religious systems that mask over the truth of Jesus with human traditions and lies.* My heart was pounding! The god of money and false religions.

There was an old Bible lying on the stand by the bed. Fumbling, I picked it up. For the second time I heard his voice, God whispered in my newly born spirit. I heard Revelation chapter 2. I was shaking. I opened the Bible and found Revelation chapter 2. As I slowly read, parts of the following verse spoke to me, "I know your works, and where you dwell, where Satan's *throne* is...where Satan dwells" (Revelation 2:13).

This verse came off the page: "Satan's throne" and "where Satan dwells." The dragon is the "beast" representing Satan's ruling power over the people of the world through the economic system, the control of money. When his power is fully manifest, no one will be able to buy or sell without the mark of the beast (the Dragon).

> And he causes all, both small and great, rich and poor, free and slave, to receive a mark on their right hand or on their foreheads, and that no one may buy or sell except one who has the mark or the name of the beast, or the number of his name. (Revelation 13:16–17 NKJV)

Secondly, another aspect of Satan's throne or deceiving power was represented by the "ugly mask," the false religious systems that mask over the truth of Jesus. Many see ugly religion and not the face of *Jesus!* As a child, I had seen "Sabbath Keeping," but not Jesus! The great whore of Revelation 17 rides the beast: The thrones of Satan— *the economic system and the Babylonian false church.* I was waking up! People see the religious mask but not Jesus. Religion does not satisfy the longing of the human heart. Countless millions have seen the ugly mask and walked away, never seeing the real living Jesus. Now they are lost in secular, materialistic, empty living.

The Satanists know this reality. The night of the Black Sabbath when they had called up enough demon power into the room, I drew these two symbols—the symbols of Satan's thrones. Somehow, this was key! They began to intensify their efforts, hoping to draw out my soul long enough to get a demon into my body. Then Satan would have had a ruling power within me; he needs bodies to carry out his will on earth.

I don't know everything they had planned for that night. Sometimes I still tremble when I consider it. I only know they wanted my soul out of my body and a demon within. I would have been in the "brotherhood of Satan," a new recruit!

Now I was on the winning team. What was next?

7
The Healing Process

The power of the resurrection continued my healing process. Even though I had lost forty-five pounds and was weak, within two days, after Jesus saved me from the pits of hell, I was up and walking. During the recovery time, God began to give me dreams and visions. He was calling me to full-time service and instructing me to go to some place that was like a camp. I could see the place in dreams and visions, but I didn't know where it was. It seemed very clear that he didn't want me in a traditional institutional church. He was calling me for my generation that clearly was lost and on the streets—those who would never go through a church door.

Now I was alive—literally from the dead—and I had met an invisible friend whose name was Jesus. I needed to learn the disciplines of hearing his voice and obeying. Some of his instructions seemed very strange and hard to understand, but I simply had to learn to obey. I recalled the first time I heard his voice in my soul concerning the drawings of the dragon and the mask. He had directed, "Turn the page over. The answer is on the back." The next time that I heard him challenged me even more.

I was gaining strength, and it was the second or third day after his healing process began in me when I heard him say, "Now take the clothes that you were wearing when you came into this room three weeks ago and burn them."

There happened to be a state mental institution only six miles from my parents' farmhouse. My natural mind began to consider that if my parents saw me burning my clothing, this could really cause some serious complications. In their understanding, I had returned from Vietnam and disappeared to Mexico. Now almost two years later, I had shown up forty-five pounds lighter, my hair falling out, brown pee, and yellow skin. What if they saw me burning my clothes?

I discreetly grabbed some matches, stuffed my clothes in a plastic bag, and quietly slipped out of the house. A creek ran through the family farm. This spot had been my favorite place when I was a boy. I loved fishing on its banks, floating downstream on the raft I had made, and camping in the summer months with my cousins and school friends. I knew every inch of the place. I left the house without being noticed and carefully walked to the bridge that crossed over the creek. The bridge wasn't far from the house, but things had changed over the years. It was wintertime, and there were no leaves on the trees; there were also fewer trees. The bridge was very visible and could be seen from the house. What if my mother saw smoke?

Next, I built a small fire under the bridge and dropped my bag of clothes onto the fire. Oh, wow! This was really weird. I was still weak, and my entire body was shaking. At last, it was done! I scattered the ashes and walked back to the house. No one saw me. It was years later when I read these verses that I understood.

> And on some have compassion, making a distinction; but others save with fear, pulling them out of the fire, hating even the garment defiled by the flesh. (Jude 1:22–23 NKJV)

My clothes were defiled. The curse of sickness and death had been upon me. My clothes were contaminated and needed to be burned.

I soon discovered I couldn't share with my family what had happened to me. I thought my dear mother would be so happy to learn how Jesus had lifted me from the gates of hell. Following the traditions of her mother, she attended the Seventh Day Adventist church. She was diligent to tithe, keep the Sabbath day, not wear earrings, and keep certain dietary laws. Therefore, I thought she would be the first to appreciate and understand what Jesus had done in my life. I finally understood and wanted her to know.

At the first opportunity, I sat down with her in the living room of the farmhouse and tried to explain. It was all very new and fresh with me. Tears streamed down my face as I tried to explain how Jesus had literally caught me. I had experienced his precious blood washing over me.

Instead of being relieved and rejoicing with me, my mother was very alarmed. She scolded me and said I should pull myself together and take control of my mind and emotions. I was hurt! I saw that it would not be wise to try to say more. At that point, I truly wondered if anyone would ever believe me.

Then I remembered the dreams. Burning in my heart was the desire to find the place I had seen in the dreams. I needed to get there. But where was that place?

A friend agreed to drive me to Dallas. I placed my small bag of clothes in his car and returned to my room to make sure I had not left anything. To my surprise, the Bible that had been on the nightstand was now lying open on the bed! I glanced down at the pages. I could only see one verse. It was as if the entire page was blacked out except for this verse: "But it has happened to them according to the true proverb: 'A dog returns to his own vomit,' and 'a sow, having washed, to her wallowing in the mire'" (2 Peter 2:22).

My heart began to pound with fear! Was I not to return to Dallas? But I couldn't just stay with my parents. My friend was waiting in the car. Shaken, I slowly walked to the car and got in. I waved goodbye to my mother and returned to Dallas.

Part Two: The Call to Discipleship

8
The Children of God

After arriving at my apartment in Dallas, it was as if all hell broke loose against me. Satan was tempting me in every way, and I was growing weaker. But where was the place I had seen in dreams and visions after Jesus saved my soul from death in hell? It was a big step to close out my apartment and leave Dallas, not knowing where I was going! I climbed into the old car that my friend had given me and started driving west. Why? I just did. I didn't know much about praying, but I talked to God and asked him to direct the car. I drove west through Fort Worth, not having any idea where I was going. I just kept heading west.

Not long after leaving Fort Worth, I encountered a hitchhiker who was standing alongside the road. He stood there in the middle of nowhere. I stopped, and he got in. "Where are you going?" he asked.

"I don't know" I answered. "Where are you headed?" I asked him.

"I don't know," he responded.

That was all. We never talked again.

Several hours passed, and it was almost sunset when I saw a sign that said something about Jesus. There was a dirt road leading off the main highway to the left. "Do you want to get out?" I asked the hitchhiker.

"No," he replied. We drove about thirty minutes down the dirt road and came to a gate. Two young men were there. They greeted us like they expected visitors, opened the gate, and we drove on over a small hill. Then I saw it; there was the camp I had seen in visions and dreams. We parked. I got out, and four young men greeted me. I began to weep and ask where I was because I had seen the place in dreams and visions. They said something about "the time had arrived for the final world harvest, and Jesus was gathering his workers."

With no further explanation, they placed their hands on me and began praying in "strange" languages. The power of God hit me, and I fell to the ground. Apparently, I went "out," and they carried me to a dormitory.

The next morning, I awoke in a bunk bed speaking in another language. The young man who had been assigned to me laughed and told me I was speaking in tongues of the Spirit. "Where am I? What is this place?"

"You are at the Children of God Texas Training Camp," he explained.

"Where's the other guy who was with me?" I asked as I looked around.

He answered, "We didn't see anyone with you and don't remember any person arriving with you."

No one who I asked had any remembrance of another person nor did they see him. He simply was not there.

Approximately 400 disciples resided at this camp. It was the time of the Jesus People Movement of the 1970s. I felt safe and comfortable at this place of discipleship. On that first day, several of the disciples said that they needed to pray to see what my Bible name was. The group began praying in tongues. "I got it. Your name is Proverbs!" one of them declared!

"Proverbs who?" I asked.

"Just Proverbs, it's a book in the Bible!"

For the next three years, Proverbs was my name. The Children of God taught that one must forsake all: name, family, country, all that one possessed and follow Jesus.

> So likewise, whoever of you does not forsake all
> that he has cannot be My disciple. (Luke 14:33)

I considered this. Jesus had forsaken all, died on the cross, and had gone into hell to rescue me. He had caught me and brought me up from the gates of hell. It seemed only right. I could be "Proverbs" and go wherever. My life was his.

The training was intense. Soon, we were sent out. Some of us were instructed to hitchhike to New York City. The plan was to witness on the streets. We stayed in New York City for several weeks and moved from street to street, sharing Jesus Christ. The next assignment was Florida. Our group of twelve then left New York in an old converted school bus and headed for Fort Lauderdale, Florida, to begin a work there. Every day, for nine months, we won souls for Jesus on the Florida beaches.

Then one day, my team leader said we were going next to Mexico City. He knew I had been there, so of course I was chosen to be a part of the team. *Oh, no!* This plan so alarmed me that my entire body began to shake after hearing the news. *Anywhere but Mexico City!* Did I really have to go back there?

A few weeks later, we were there, on the streets daily. My team had memorized thirty Bible verses in Spanish. They were basic salvation verses we were to use. One night, we were on the street witnessing at the Glorieta de Insurgentes. This area is a popular tourist destination known for its museums, art galleries, restaurants, and nearby cafes. I was talking to a young man about Jesus when suddenly, I had a strange feeling that someone was behind me. I turned, and there stood Grant! I recognized those same eyes. He greeted me like an old friend. Then began the warfare.

He started telling me how he was with 3,000 witches and warlocks from Los Angeles County and that they would win! I was shaken. But I knew enough now and began to quote scriptures to him. It was tense. How did he find me? Mexico City has twelve million people! I quoted the scripture: "I must be about my Father's business." He replied, "The same." He was about his father's business. He left!

This astonishing harassment continued. On one occasion, I went to the Mexico City airport alone. I was booked for an early morning flight to Mazatlán; the Children of God were planning to open a work there. After getting my boarding pass, I decided to grab a cup of coffee at "Wings." The place was almost empty. I was enjoying drinking my coffee when who else but Grant came in. He sat two empty tables down from me and began intently staring at me. I was still young in the Lord and battling with fear, so instead of addressing his presence with "What are you doing here?" I paid and got out of there. Grant followed me all the way to the security gate.

9
The Departure

Six months passed in Mexico City with the Children of God. I was maturing in my ability to listen to God. I was troubled in that he was telling me to get out of the Children of God movement! I was feeling increasingly uncomfortable traveling with Watchman, the leader. He had some very noticeable flaws, but that was not the only reason for my discomfort. I knew in my spirit that something was not right with them.

For weeks, the Holy Spirit had been prompting me to leave. But where would I go? This was a monumental step of faith for me. I had forsaken everything including my name. Materially speaking, I had nothing apart from the Children of God movement. I had grown to love everyone in it; however, I was no longer at peace in this situation. The Holy Spirit continued to be persistent with me. I really didn't understand; it didn't make sense to me. I wrestled continually with the awareness that I had to go. It wouldn't be until years later that I would clearly understand. The Children of God had taken some wrong turns and had diverted into serious error. They had become a cult that progressively degenerated and became extremely controlling.

I was in a really difficult trial: Where would I go? Where would I live? How would I eat? The Children of God system was communal living. I had nothing of my own except my Bible, a change of clothes, a sleeping bag, and a backpack. What was it about México City? First it had been the Satanists; now how to "escape" from The Children of God?

One morning, before anyone was awake, I grabbed my possessions and quietly slipped out the door of the large house we had rented. At first, I ran; then I began walking and walking. Eventually, I came to a large park, Parque Hundido, in the middle of Colonia Roma in Mexico City. I sat down on a bench, and throughout the day, I prayed and considered what I might do next. The hours went by, and I sat alone with no place to go and nothing to do but find a safe place to sleep. I was a stranger and pilgrim on the earth. The nights can get cold in Mexico City. I decided to walk through the park and look around. Where would I spend the night?

Eventually, I decided where to roll out my sleeping bag. I spent my first night with "no place to lay my head," except on the ground under some bushes. I felt peace and a sense of fellowship with Jesus that I had never felt before. It was just me and him. I was in the same situation as he had been. "Foxes have dens and birds have nests, but the Son of Man has no place to lay his head" (Luke 9:58). I was experiencing the "fellowship of his sufferings" (Philippians 3:10).

Where would my Father lead me next? What was I to do? How would I survive? I had no money, nothing to eat, one change of clothes, a small Bible, and the inward presence of Jesus.

10
The Plumed Serpent

Morning came quickly.

I sat for a while on my favorite park bench, meditating on the Word, praying and endeavoring to strengthen my faith. Thank God there was a bathroom in the park. Throughout the day, I was fighting fear and hunger. I knew about fasting, but this was different.

Another day was going by. The park was large and very beautifully landscaped. There seemed to be a safe family environment about it. As I walked, prayed, and fought the fear that was trying to overwhelm me, I discovered a small police station in the park. A couple of laid-back policemen were milling about. Behind the building, I saw a couple of large trash barrels. Realizing that if I climbed up on the barrels, I could easily crawl onto the flat roof, I waited, and when darkness set in and all was quiet, I carefully made my way onto the rooftop. No one saw me!

On the roof lay some piles of broom straw used for sweeping the walkways in the park. Perfect! Sleeping under the bushes was damp, cold, and perhaps dangerous. This was much better. I could hear the policemen talking down below; they had no idea that I was on the roof above them.

Prayers of thanksgiving and rejoicing welled up in my heart for this provision, but I felt ever conscious that I was living through a very strange trial. At times, it all seemed so unbelievable, but it was real! I had almost been killed once in Mexico City by Satanists, and now I found myself in another difficult situation. However, this time, I had a helper—the Holy Spirit. I wasn't alone. I was now actively participating in an intensive, disciplined school of learning on how to listen and follow. The verse in Romans 8:14 rolled over in my mind, "For as many as are led by the Spirit of God, these are the sons of God." This verse was my lesson in practical training on how to be led.

Early the next morning, I climbed very quietly off the roof. No one saw me. Bravo! Another day passed in the park, and my situation was becoming even more desperate. Then I remembered something. When I was attending the university, I became acquainted with some Aztec Indians who sat in front of the university, selling their artwork. These Indians came from the state of Guerrero, and I loved them. Back then, I had visited their village and stayed there for days at a time. I became especially acquainted with one family—Sabino, his wife, Juana, and their children.

The village was located in the mountains between Iguala and Chilpancingo, Guerrero. The state of Guerrero is located almost straight south of Mexico City, bordering the Pacific Ocean, with the famous tourist capital of Acapulco on its coast. I prayed for help from the Holy Spirit and then hitchhiked to the village where my Aztec friends lived.

I connected with Sabino and his family and loved being there with them. Sabino and I hunted for iguanas, and I learned to shoot his musket loaded with very small rocks for buckshot: this was 1971. Juana made delicious tortillas, and the children were fascinated with my beard and long hair. It felt like home in many ways. During my earlier visits, when I was first attending the university and didn't know Jesus, I had considered that perhaps this was a place to find a wife and live here with these people in their very simple, primitive culture.

These people still spoke Náhuatl, the native Azteca language; however, my friend Sabino spoke both Náhuatl and Spanish. Juana spoke in her native tongue and knew about as much Spanish as I did. We tried to communicate and succeeded. Somehow, the language of love from the heart was working.

Burning in me was the desire to share my experiences and the reality of Jesus with them. I would spend hours trying to explain how

God had sent his Son to bring us into a close relationship with him. I wanted them to know the love and the reality of Jesus. They were very patient with me, but gradually, I discerned that this sleepy little village of adobe homes, dirt floors, no plumbing, and no electricity was more complicated than I had first thought.

It is vital to understand that Catholicism in many areas of Mexico is a blend of Catholic traditions and paganism. Praying to saints depicted by statues works perfectly with the idolatry associated with heathenism. Although this idolatrous form of Catholicism existed on the surface, there was an undercurrent that ran in the hearts of these people. They were still worshipping the plumed serpent god of the ancient Aztecs (Quetzalcoatl). Perhaps having narrowly escaped from the Satanists and now being filled with the Holy Spirit, my senses were sharpened enough to know that there was something deeper going on.

Often late at night, I listened to the rhythm of drums playing on the mountaintop across the river piercing the night. The spirit of the drums caused me to feel ill at ease, and it was impossible to sleep on these nights. This native religion was not just an art expression; at least, for some, it was their source of worship. Many of the locals were engaged in painting beautiful birds in trees on a type of pressed bark paper. They sold these paintings to tourists in Acapulco and other places. However, what appeared to be beautiful birds were not birds at all, in some cases, but rather winged, feathered serpents. I recognized that the serpents on the bark paper paintings were representative of the winged "ancient serpent" who had been cursed and made to crawl in the dust. "On your belly you shall go, and you shall eat dust all the days of your life" (Genesis 3:14).

The Holy Spirit began to show me in scripture about the battle ahead.

> For which of you, intending to build a tower, does not sit down first and count the cost, whether he has enough to finish it. (Luke 14:28)

> Or what king, going to make war against
> another king, does not sit down first and con-
> sider whether he is able with ten thousand to
> meet him who comes against him with twenty
> thousand? (Luke 14:31)

I was not ready for this battle, and I realized it.

Sabino and Juana were dear friends, but there were others in the village who were not so friendly. I knew I was called to serve Jesus and share what he had done for me, but this was too great a challenge. I could not "just live" in the village, keeping quiet, with the call that was on my life. I also recognized that I was not ready to engage in this battle yet. I would have to go. But where?

11
The Assurance

One midafternoon, I told Sabino and Juana goodbye and headed toward the road. I was standing alongside that road with tears running down my face as I waited for the third-class bus. I had no idea where to go. Then it happened. I heard the audible voice of God! He said to me, "I will raise up a work in Kansas that will support you on this field."

I was totally shocked. A work in Kansas? I had forgotten about Kansas! I glanced at my watch; it was 3:00 p.m. God had sent a Word to me! There was no question about it.

To have a Word straight from God is the greatest treasure. It produces faith and will accomplish the purpose for which it was sent.

> As rain comes down, and snow from heaven, and do not return there, but water the earth, And make it bring forth and bud, That it may give seed to the sower And bread to the eater, So shall My Word be that goes forth from My mouth; It shall not return to Me void, But it shall accomplish what I please, And shall prosper in the thing for which I sent it. (Isaiah 55:10–11)

Then just after he spoke to me, in a flash of revelation that my mind's eye can still see, I saw the dark principalities over this region, the fallen angels that have ruled over these people for generations.

I knew that it would require an army of intercessors and seasoned workers to break open this area for the Gospel.

I boarded an old bus for Iguala, which was the closest city. From there, for some unknown reason, I continued on the road to Taxco. A few kilometers after leaving Iguala, I noticed a Catholic church perched on a high hill about a kilometer or so off the road. I trudged up the dusty road leading to the church, and as I arrived, I met a priest who was just leaving. I asked him if he had a place where I could pray and fast for a few days. He was very accommodating and gave me a room off the sanctuary in an enclosed garden area. He then told me he was leaving for a few days.

Even though I wanted to fast, each day, a lady and her little boy brought me something to eat. This was all unexpected. Then, about ten o'clock on the third night, while I was resting on a cot in an otherwise empty room, something amazing happened. Four angels descended into the middle of the room. Did I see them with my natural eyes? I really don't know. I just know that I saw them and can still see them when I think about it. They had arms and wings.

The four of them locked their arms and formed what I would describe as a pinwheel. Then each of them extended his left wing, and they began to move in a circular motion. The feathers of each extended wing very lightly brushed over my bare back, moving from my waist up. As their feathers brushed over my back, I was filled with indescribable glory. There was a tremendous strength that came into me. I recalled the following scriptures:

> And he was there in the wilderness forty days, tempted by Satan, and was with the wild beasts; and the angels ministered to him. (Mark 1:13)

> Speaking of angels, "Are they not all ministering spirits sent forth to minister for those who will inherit salvation?" (Hebrews 1:14)

Then they were gone! The experience is hard to describe, but it greatly strengthened and encouraged me. That next morning, I left for Mexico City and returned to the same park. There was no other familiar place to go!

Around 2:00 a.m. in the park, I was praying and literally crying out to God. I was no longer on the rooftop of the police station but on the lawn partly hidden among the gardens. I could not see him with my natural eyes, but Jesus came to me. It was a clear, powerful visitation. I was on my knees at this point and could sense him standing in front of me. He communicated to me portions of his Word from Matthew 10:6–10:

> But go rather to the lost sheep… And as you go, preach, saying, "The kingdom of heaven is at hand." Heal the sick, cleanse the lepers, raise the dead, cast out demons. Freely you have received, freely give.

> Provide neither gold nor silver nor copper in your money belts. (Matthew 10:9)

> [n]or bag for your journey, nor two tunics, nor sandals, nor staffs; for a worker is worthy of his food. (Matthew 10:10)

Then his Word came to me from Matthew chapter 6.

> Therefore I say to you, do not worry about your life, what you will eat or what you will drink; or about your body, what you will put on. Is not life more than food and the body more than clothing? (Matthew 6:25)

> Look at the birds of the air, for they neither sow nor reap nor gather into barns; yet your heavenly Father feeds them. Are you not of more value than they? (Matthew 6:26)

But seek first the kingdom of God and his righteousness, and all these things shall be added to you. (Matthew 6:33)

Therefore do not worry about tomorrow, for tomorrow will worry about its own things. Sufficient for the day is its own trouble. (Matthew 6:34)

Suddenly, Jesus was gone! I was crying. He had given me direct instructions! Besides the word about Kansas, which he had spoken to me alongside the road in Guerrero, he had now given me another direct word. The experience filled me with great awe. I glanced down at the ground, and there in front of me lay a pair of baby shoes. They looked new—little shoes made of leather and bronze colored; they were meant to give me a message.

Picking them up, I placed them in my hands and I heard distinctly, "You gotta be a baby!"

In the Children of God, we sang this song frequently, "Except a man be converted and become as a child he cannot enter the kingdom of heaven; 'you gotta be a baby.'" I began to cry, and at the same time began dancing and rejoicing in the park! He was with me and had commissioned me!

Following Jesus is simply a matter of trusting him like a little child and doing what he is asking. He has sent the person of the Holy Spirit, the "other comforter," to guide us. Jesus had spoken. I had my orders. I would go to work and stop worrying about what I was supposed to do, what I would eat, and where I would live. I would simply look for lost sheep and do what he said to do. Those baby shoes remained in my backpack for the next three years. Every time I was in doubt (or hungry), I would look at those baby shoes and remember the divine moment they were given to me.

12
And Now We Are Four

The next day in "my" park was very different. As I was looking for "lost sheep," I found a young man by the name of Lucas. I led Lucas to Jesus. He accepted the Lord as we sat on the grass. He was crying so much that the police thought we were "loaded." They pushed us into a police car and began to rough us up, wanting the marijuana! We didn't have any of that but something better! They eventually gave up and let us go. Lucas was in his last year at the National University, studying business administration, but he was lost just like I had been. I told Lucas to go home and tell his parents goodbye and forsake all. I would see him tomorrow. He did it!

After Lucas left, I was walking down the street and came to an open-air restaurant that I had never seen before. The lady in charge called to me and told me to sit down. She then brought me half a chicken with fries and a salad! I quietly asked the Lord for something to drink. The lady who stood with her back to me washing dishes called to me, "What would you like to drink?"

When I finished that great meal, I thanked this precious lady, and she replied, "*De nada* (It's nothing)!" I left, rejoicing, greatly encouraged. Jesus had done it! The workman is worthy of his food. I could do this! I was walking in faith according to what he had told me.

Next, I came upon Julio in the park. He was playing his guitar and had wandered from Honduras, Central America, to Mexico. Like me, he had studied architecture and not finished the course. He was more of a musician than an architect, and he was lost just like Lucas had been. Julio spoke English as well as his native Spanish language. His heart broke as I shared the Word with him. He then gave his life to Jesus.

Both Julio and Lucas were addicted to marijuana, and both were delivered. They were totally set free of the addiction. The next day, Julio and Lucas returned to the park. Now we were three. We sat on my bench and read the Word of God out loud. As we were reading the Book of Matthew, we came to chapter 4, and something happened. Verses 15 and 16 stood out on the page and shot into my heart.

> [B]y the way of the sea ("by the way of the sea" I heard in my spirit) the Jordan, Galilee of the Gentiles. (Matthew 4:15)

> The people who sat in darkness have seen a great light, and upon those who sat in the region and shadow of death Light has dawned. (Matthew 4:16)

I immediately asked Lucas and Julio, "Where is the sea?"
They gave the most obvious answer, "Acapulco!"
I said, "Let's go!"
We walked and hitchhiked from Mexico City to the outskirts of Acapulco. That trip lasted several days. Finally, when we reached Acapulco, having ridden the final stretch in an enclosed truck that was hauling furniture, the driver informed us the ride was over. He could not transport us into Acapulco in the back of his truck, so we gave up our "easy chairs" and got out at an intersection. While standing there, we saw a dirt road that led to the south. If we continued on the highway, we would end up in Acapulco. What were we to do? For at least five hours, I sought the Lord about which way to go. When I think about it, I can still feel the affliction of soul that I carried during those hours.

Julio was sitting in the shade under a tree, playing his guitar and writing new songs of worship. Lucas was wandering in the coconut grove. Then alongside the road, he found a puppy, which he claimed as his. Now we were four! The visual of us must have been quite a sight. We stood at this intersection, one of those divine intersections that happens during the course of life. At last, I felt I knew the answer, and we started walking south. For two months, we walked south! Eventually, we arrived in Puerto Escondido. I could never have imagined what God had in mind and the importance of this walk.

As we walked, we entered small towns. Julio would play his guitar, we would sing, and a crowd would gather around us. With our long hair and beards and now a dog, we drew a crowd without much effort. We would endeavor to preach the kingdom of God (what little we knew) and pray for the sick. Oftentimes, some lady would invite us to her house to pray for someone. Then we would be fed and given a place to stay. It was all very amazing.

While walking, Julio, Lucas, and I memorized Bible verses: two verses each day. We read the Bible out loud to each other as we sat alongside the road waiting for a ride. There was very little traffic, and when we did get a ride, it was short. There still were no bridges over some of the rivers, only pontoon boats that could ferry small vehicles. Every night, we would watch and pray. We took turns of two hours each. We would frequently camp by a river and build a campfire for light so we could read during our watches. The river was also a great place for bathing, and at times, there was no other water to drink. One such night, during my watch, I discovered Mark 15:16: "He who believes and is baptized will be saved; but he who does not believe will be condemned."

Neither Julio, Lucas, nor I were baptized. The Children of God movement had overlooked water baptism. Even though I had not learned all the doctrine on baptism, I woke up Julio and Lucas and baptized them. Then the both of them baptized me, Julio on one side, Lucas on the other. We were on a new level. What a great school we were in!

13
The Peace Child: Brother Polo

We had been on this journey for weeks, and now we were approximately 150 miles south of Acapulco. It was my turn to hitchhike. As I was sitting under a shade tree alongside the road, waiting for a ride, I looked up and saw a man running toward me. He was the perfect picture of the original "campesino"—white pants and shirt with a wide sombrero and a mustache. It seems as if there was light all around him as he approached me.

He took my hand, lifting me up, and insisted that we come to his house. I was a little frightened and told him I would have to talk with my friends.

The man's name was Leopoldo Ruiz Cruz, but he introduced himself to us as "Brother Polo." He had been born again about a year before. A missionary passing through the area had led Polo to the Lord. The missionary had given him a cassette player and a tape with the Gospel message. Now Polo was going from place to place, playing the cassette tape to whoever would listen. As Polo was playing the tape for a lady in a small store near where I was sitting, the lady told him he should talk to those "three bums" over there alongside the road. She told him we were like him! Her words shot into his heart, and an excited Polo came running. He and his wife, Cata, were the only believers in the town of San José Del Progreso. Polo insisted that we come immediately to his house.

Julio, Lucas, and I accepted Polo's invitation. Polo lived in a one-room stick house with a dirt floor and a palm thatched roof along with his wife, three sons, and his mother-in-law. We stayed with them for a couple of weeks and fell in love with Polo and Cata. We gave him the Bible name of "Apocalipsis" (Spanish name for the book of Revelation) because he was such a revelation of Jesus. They were poor in possessions but rich in faith.

Many times, there were only dried tortillas with salt to eat. Yet, we were the happiest people on the planet. We read scripture together and shared with Polo the call to discipleship from Matthew chapter 10 and Matthew chapter 6. Subsequently, he gave his plot of land to his oldest son and also gave away his machete. Polo became a full-time evangelist for many years. Eventually, a church birthed in his home. It was this beginning that grew into the church of San José del Progreso today.

Cata's mother was lying on a bed made of sticks and had been ill for many days. They were convinced she was dying. After we were there for some time, helping Polo gather firewood and build his kitchen, Julio felt a great compassion rise up in his heart for this dying lady. One afternoon, he boldly walked into the palm hut where she was lying, took her by the hand, and commanded her in the name of Jesus to get up. She got up, was healed, and lived in good health for many years after that!

The bond that formed between us lasted for years and became "the door of entry" for mission work into this region of southern Mexico. When Jesus sent out the first disciples, they were instructed to look for the home where they found peace, the place that "is worthy." Therefore, Polo became the "peace child" (the worthy place where our peace rested). This was one of the main hidden reasons for the journey down the southern coast of Mexico in 1971. It was to find what some call "the peace child." This was the open door.

> But whatever house you enter, first say, "Peace to this house." And if a son of peace is there, your peace will rest on it; if not it will return to you. (Luke 10:5–6)

The time eventually came to say goodbye to Polo and Cata to move on in this Holy Spirit journey. After our "goodbyes," Julio, Lucas, and I began our return journey up the coast to Acapulco and then to Mexico City. Along the way, there were miraculous provisions. We arrived in Acapulco at the same juncture where two months earlier, the Holy Spirit had directed us to travel south down this dirt road marked as route "200." At that time, we could not understand the importance of having found "the peace child." Nor did we have understanding of the importance and significance of the journey we had just made.

In the years to come, the eternal destiny of thousands of people would be changed because of this walk down the coastline of southern Mexico. We walk by faith! Remember, Julio, Lucas and I had been reading the book of Matthew, sitting on a park bench in Mexico City. Faith comes by "hearing." We had made this journey because of a Word the Holy Spirit had caused me to "hear:" [b]y the way of the sea… The people who sat in darkness have seen a great light, And upon those who sat in the region and shadow of death Light has dawned" (Matt. 4:15–16).

Now we were simply, hot, tired, dusty, and hungry after riding for several hours on a flatbed truck. At the time, the journey did not seem all that significant to us. Perhaps we can imagine how father Abraham felt dwelling in tents and walking through the land of promise. He could not have known what his walk in that land would mean for thousands of people for thousands of years. As for our walk, at the time of this writing (2019), approximately 12,000 people from the formally unreached tribes of southern Mexico are now redeemed, alive unto God and members of sixty-seven churches the Lord has enabled us to establish in Southern Mexico.

Julio, Lucas, and I sat on the curb. It was almost sundown. We prayed for something to eat. Within ten minutes, a man approached, walking briskly toward us. He carried a tray with an assortment of tacos and enchiladas. He handed us the tray and, without another word, said, "Here. Eat." He gave us the tray with the food and quickly walked on.

Cata and Polo

14

The Teepee: A School in the Wilderness

When we arrived in Mexico City, we were on the streets. It wasn't that we were university dropouts or part of the hippy culture of that day. There was an intense, divine training taking place. We were, in the literal sense, "strangers and pilgrims on this earth" (Hebrews 11:13). As Jesus said of the early disciples, "They are not of this world, just as I am not of this world" (John 17:16). To some, this may seem like foolishness or difficult to understand, but we were learning to listen and obey. It was a rare intense training that would serve me for many years.

Some days went by, then a lady who owned a camping equipment store gave Julio a used camping tent. We took the tent and went to the mountains of La Marquesa between México City and Toluca. We found a great spot to pitch our tent in a meadow within the pine forest where a mountain stream flowed close by. This location was only about an hour's walk from the highway. The mountain air and natural beauty was a welcome change from Mexico City. We would daily read the Word together, pray, and worship. It was heavenly.

We became acquainted with a lady named Maria who had escaped from Cuba with her three daughters. They were Christians. Maria would drive up in her little car with her daughters and bring us food. She would park the car as close as possible and walk the rest of the way.

The tent that Julio acquired was old and left much to be desired. It leaked and was too small. Julio, Lucas, and I fasted and prayed for a day about what we should do. Each of us in a very personal way "got it" that we should build a three-story teepee-shaped structure on this mountain. It's true, we were in a national park. But for us, this park was home. We hiked around the mountain until we agreed on a spot to build our dwelling. Julio and I, being architects of a sort, perceived how the structure would be built. Lucas had a vision that the structure was transparent.

We had made friends with the shepherds who grazed their sheep in the upper meadows. They loaned us shovels, horses, ropes, axes, and all kinds of tools. We were all set. When the work was just getting started, Lucas decided he should go tell his parents where he had been and what the Lord had done for him. We prayed with him and sent him away with the promise that he would return. Days went by, and Lucas did not return.

Julio loved Lucas like a little brother and would weep as he prayed for him. Finally, Julio got discouraged. He told me one morning, "Proverbs (this was still my name given by the Children of God), I don't think this is my ministry to be digging in the side of this mountain."

I replied, "What do you mean this isn't your ministry?" We discussed the matter throughout the morning. I pleaded with him not to leave. When I last saw him, he was trudging down the mountain with his backpack and guitar strapped on his back. I cried!

In the early morning on the same day before Julio left, I had walked the beautiful mountain trails. The verse I memorized that morning was Hebrews 12:1: "Therefore we also, since we are surrounded by so great a cloud of witnesses, let us lay aside every weight, and the sin which so easily ensnares us, and let us run with endurance the race that is set before us."

This verse speaks of a "great cloud" of witnesses around us, but now with Lucas and Julio both gone, it seemed that I was totally alone. The afternoon passed. It was raining and cold, and I was living in a national forest in a leaky tent with nothing but a small Bible and a change of clothes. Sometimes I cried. What had happened to

Lucas? And Julio? He had said he was going to play his guitar and sing his songs to people. We three had shared the same vision. We had planned to build a structure on this mountain from which we would do our outreaches.

Mercifully, I fell asleep. Suddenly, in the middle of the night, I woke up with a start and sat up while praying loudly in tongues. All around me, I saw horses, chariots, and angels! The great cloud of witnesses! Then I lay back down and instantly fell asleep. The next morning, when I opened my eyes, I recalled what happened in the night. Was it real? My mind began to doubt. But at that moment, I heard the verse I had memorized the day before:

> Therefore we also, since we are surrounded by so great a cloud of witnesses, let us lay aside every weight, and the sin which so easily ensnares us, and let us run with endurance the race that is set before us. (Hebrews 12:1)

I had seen it! I was not alone at all! There truly was a great cloud of witnesses around me. They were here with me. I rejoiced, picked up my shovel, and began to dig with renewed faith.

I can't remember how many days passed by until Julio returned with a young man, Joshua. Joshua was the name Julio gave him. He had led this young man to the Lord. Joshua was from Honduras and was studying in Mexico to be a doctor. Julio went and got Joshua. The three of us began to work hard building the place. For six months, we worked. Joshua grew to love the Lord and became a true disciple.

One day, as were working, we looked up, and there was Lucas. He was back, but something was wrong. When Lucas had tried to tell his parents about his faith and all that had happened with him, his parents placed him in a mental institution! They thought he had lost his mind. In the hospital, he was given electric shocks, pills, and terrible treatment. There were red blotches on his neck where he told us they had given him shock therapy. Lucas went on to explain how the people in the hospital were Satanists and had tried to force him to deny his faith. He was spaced out and mixed up.

We cried and prayed over him. He cried a lot, and often, he just stood there, staring, lost in a world of his own. For a few days, Lucas would be all right, and then he would wander off. It was all so sad. Finally, we lost him and never saw him again.

During the time we were building the teepee, we never stopped witnessing. We led some families to the Lord who lived in the town of La Marquesa, which is located on the superhighway between México City and Toluca. These families made their living selling barbecue lamb, goat, and beef tacos. They grazed their animals on the mountain meadows. We held weekly meetings with them in their homes. It wasn't long before the Forrestal police also got saved! Since we were building a structure on government land in a national forest, this worked to our advantage. We needed the favor of the Forrestal police. They allowed us to cut pine trees, but only pines that were dead. We promised to obey.

Our tent was about an hour walk from the highway. Our routine was to walk down the mountain to La Marquesa and the highway to hitch a ride into Mexico City to evangelize. We were leading young people to the Lord in México City.

For almost two years, we lived in this mountain teepee we had carved into the side of the mountain. The interior of the structure had three levels. At times, up to twenty-five people were living in this amazing place. They were from Honduras, Oklahoma, New Jersey and, of course, Mexico. We were reading, worshipping, praying, and going in and out on "faith" mission trips according to Matthew chapter 10. It was the most amazing experience. We were in "Bible school" without knowing it.

We began each morning with praise and Bible reading. The chores followed—cutting firewood, cooking and cleaning. By noon each day, we were ready to go soul-winning. We would go two by two or sometimes in groups. None of us had any income, but we were living and moving about by faith miraculously. After several months, close to 100 people would often come to the mountain on the weekends to worship and hear the Word. Our followers came from México City and La Marquesa.

Part Three:
The Journey
Continues

15
The Call to Honduras

Julio left for his home in Honduras. He shared Jesus with his friends and returned to Mexico with six of them who received the Lord. After a few months, two of these disciples decided that they were going to read the Book of Acts out loud throughout the day, and when they finished, we would pray for them and send them to Honduras to win their friends. They finished around midafternoon. We prayed, rejoiced, and sent them on their way. Months later, we got a notice from these two disciples that a number of their university friends had given their lives to the Lord. They asked if I would come to Honduras. Julio remained behind.

I traveled to Honduras, planning to stay only a few weeks and then return to the mountain. Instead, I lived in Honduras for a year and six months. I never returned to the mountain teepee. Note: Julio later graduated from the prestigious Berklee School of Music in Boston, Massachusetts. He was the Director of Music at the National University in Tegucigalpa, Honduras, for thirty years. Nelson Guerra, one of the disciples who read the Book of Acts out loud before returning to Honduras, is today an apostle with a network of thirty-four churches in eight different countries.

Upon arrival in Honduras, some of the disciples and I went to a river to baptize the new converts. That evening, the Holy Spirit fell on them in a powerful way. This sparked a movement in Tegucigalpa, Honduras. God was pouring out his Spirit. Within a few weeks, there were approximately ninety university-age disciples attending our meetings.

A wealthy Arabian family (a mother and her three daughters) in Tegucigalpa accepted Jesus. The father had been killed. This family owned an estate a few kilometers out of Tegucigalpa. The mother and her daughters insisted that the main group of disciples should live at this estate. It was abandoned. When the father was living, this facility had been used by government officials for parties and gatherings.

Fifteen of us moved into the estate. It was a remarkable provision. Now we had a base. We cleaned it up and developed a style of life similar to the mountain at La Marquesa in Mexico. By noon each day, we would go into Tegucigalpa to witness at the university. Many of the youth who were accepting Jesus were from upper-class families. We began to gather these new converts and hold discipleship meetings with them in the backyards of their homes. The parents of these "on-fire" youth would watch from the sidelines, slightly puzzled and slightly glad.

The daughter of one of these upper-class families gave her life to the Lord. She surrendered her heart totally and was very fervent. Her father was the Honduran ambassador to Germany at the time. The family being traditionally Catholic. Her father was not pleased with his daughter's decision. She learned that her father was coming to Honduras to take her to Germany, so she fled to San Pedro Sula, Honduras, to a friend's house to hide. I knew absolutely nothing about this.

One day, this girl's mother called three of us to her house. The mother accused us of taking her daughter as a hostage. Two witches sat in her living room, helping the mother to cross-examine us, trying to find out the daughter's location. When we could give no answers, the mother clapped her hands in an authoritarian way, and two policemen came out of a side room and took me to jail.

At the jail, I was stripped down to my underwear and locked in a cell with fifteen other prisoners. The cell was a small concrete box, about six feet wide and twelve feet long, with iron bars for a door. There was no toilet and no beds, just a concrete floor with concrete walls and fleas. A gallon can on the floor outside the iron bars of the door provided a place to urinate. That bucket was almost always running over, and one was permitted an escort for only one toilet visit per day. There was no provision of food or water for the prisoners, except a watery tin cup of coffee early each morning. Any food had to be brought in by someone on the outside, a friend or family member.

When I laid my bare body down on the concrete floor, my head touched one wall and my feet the other wall. This was Honduras Central America; the tropical heat plus the odor in the cell was overwhelming.

After the initial shock, my emotions calmed, and I knew Jesus was with me. I hadn't done anything wrong. The young woman who had fled from her father was twenty-one years of age. I didn't know where she was or that she had left Tegucigalpa. To my surprise, Marcos, the guard, brought me a sandwich and some water. Some of the disciples were taking care of me! I told him to tell them that there were sixteen of us. Later, water and sixteen sandwiches arrived. I instructed all my fellow prisoners to sit on the floor around the walls. I prayed, and then each one opened his sandwich, for inside each sandwich was a paper with a Bible verse or a note of encouragement written on it! They each read their notes out loud. This could get good!

Four days and nights, I was locked up in this concrete box of a jail. The guard eventually let me have my Bible. The prisoners showed me great respect, and we became friends.

Then it happened. Marco, the guard, released me. After dressing, I went with him to the office of the "comandante." The comandante ordered everyone to leave the room. He then told me the "powers that be" wanted to deport me. The comandante was under pressure. However, he gave me some private advice. He told me to take the bus to El Salvador, spend the night, and then return. In that way, I could renew my papers to be in Honduras, yet he would have no direct involvement. He gave me a handshake and wished me well.

I made the journey to El Salvador and returned. Some months later, we were confronted with another trial. We were informed that we had to leave our base, the estate where we were living. The dear lady who owned the property along with her daughters came to see us. With tears in her eyes, she explained something to us. She had learned of a plot to put marijuana on the property, which would

73

cause for some of us to be arrested. It would cost a lot of money to get us out of jail. We would have to leave.

The Holy Spirit had been warning us that something was wrong. We closed the property, packed our backpacks, and left. We understood that "all things work together for good," but where were we to go?

Starting at the central market in Tegucigalpa, we caught an old bus that traveled into the mountains. At a point, we disembarked and began walking. We had no idea where we were going. We just kept walking and following our peace. We found ourselves in the pine trees on a dirt road. As we walked, I noticed an American Christian school to the left of the road, "Academia de los Pinares (Academy of the Pines)." How mysterious are his ways? My wife-to-be, Susan Ruth Rohrer, was teaching at the school.

This school was founded by the Mennonites for their mission-ary children. It still strives today to provide a high-quality, Christian, bilingual education with integrated biblical principles. The school draws embassy people, parents who desire their children to be taught morals and discipline, and US military families.

We continued to walk until we reached the end of the road. We arrived at the beautiful mountain village of Peregrino (meaning pilgrim). We found an empty adobe house by a stream with some strawberry fields alongside it. When we inquired, we discovered that the man who owned the house and the field was crippled due to a stroke. His wife gladly allowed us to stay in the house if we would take care of the strawberries. The people of Peregrino grew flowers, vegetables, and fruit.

An old school bus with license plates from Dade County, Florida, was the local transportation. The old bus lumbered up and down the mountain twice a day to the market in Tegucigalpa. It was on this bus that I would meet my wife, Sue.

We adapted well to our new lifestyle, caring for the strawberry field. I would give massages every day to the man who had a stroke because the muscles in his right leg and arm were atrophying. Over time, with prayer and hard work, I was able to get him out of bed and walk him.

One day, the plain clothes police or narcotic agents "supposedly" came looking for us. They found us and beat up two of the guys, trying to get them to "confess" where the drugs were. A few weeks later, they returned. This time, we began to worship and pray as they stood watching us. Then a tremendous rainstorm hit. They ran for cover and never returned. It was true, there had been a plot against us.

We traveled up and down the mountain, caring for our disciples in Tegucigalpa. However, there was no transportation at night, so how could we hold evening meetings? We had lost our base and were engaged in a level of spiritual attack that we had not experienced before.

God continued moving in a mighty way. We began to gather the disciples at the home of the woman who had originally let us stay at her estate. However, I was getting frustrated; there was not enough room here. We divided the believers into three groups: new, medium, and old (in the Lord). But the lack of space was still a hindrance. We could not go on this way.

One evening, during one of the gatherings, I went outside and began to pray for a larger place. As I prayed, I got a vision of the Union Church building several blocks down the street. I understood clearly that we were to meet in that facility.

Union Church happened to be a congregation of cold, traditionally wealthy people. However, God had sent a missionary couple by the name of Ed and Gloria King to them. Ed and Gloria were Spirit-filled Mennonites. They were also Susan Rohrer's pastors. However, at that time, I knew none of this.

I went back in the meeting and told two of the guys that I had a vision and that the Union Church would be our new place. They were in total disbelief and remarked, "That's crazy, Proverbs!" But they went with me anyway. It was about eight o'clock that evening when we walked into this very cold, traditional prayer meeting. We sat in the back pew, praying and waiting until it finished. Ed King was leading the group. At last, he acknowledged us. In my bold assurance, I told the group that we were leading a bunch of youth who were gathered up the street and that God had given me a vision; we were to use their building. Oh! Silence!

Anyway, God worked it out. An amazing youth work began in Union Church under the care of Ed and Gloria. That work became what is called "*Amor Viviente* (Living Love)." This gathering manifested a powerful move of God. Hundreds of people were saved, and churches were planted throughout Honduras and the US. The work continues to this day.

16
Susan Ruth Rohrer

As I traveled up and down the mountain on the old school bus, I met Sue. She had taken the bus to the Academia de Los Pinares. We visited. Sue asked me to speak to the Thursday night staff Bible study and to her eighth-grade Bible class. She also invited me to an evening meal with all the staff of Academia.

Sue's Story

How did a Lancaster County, Pennsylvania, Mennonite farm girl get to Tegucigalpa, Honduras? How did I happen to be on the market bus climbing the curvy mountain road, sitting across the aisle from this kind, warm-eyed, young man carrying a Bible? I had seen him on another trip up the mountain to our school complex, but he was in the back, and I near the front. He had been engaged with his open Bible with another passenger, obviously sharing the Word with them. This time, we greeted each other before getting on the bus and were able to get acquainted.

The hour-long ride gave him time to share how "pleading the blood of Jesus" as he was plunging into hell saved and healed him. His life was not his own now but rather dedicated to following the Lord in wherever and whatever he was doing. The authenticity penetrated my heart.

I invited him to our Thursday night staff Bible study and to my eighth-grade homeroom Bible class. This was "Book of Acts" stuff, and I was captivated. To meet someone who was alive, literally because of calling on the name of Jesus, resonated deeply within me.

Missions were definitely a family affair. My great-uncle was the first chairman of the Eastern Mennonite Mission Board. One of the first missionaries sent from our area to East Africa, Clyde Shenk, was from our home church of Millersville Mennonite. My favorite aunt became a missionary nurse to Honduras, Central America, when I was about ten years old. Her stories of pioneer nursing in the tropics of LaCeiba, Honduras, held all twenty of us cousins captivated. She was my hero.

Duane continues…

My time in Honduras was coming to an end. I released the work we had begun to Ed and Gloria King. The Word that God had spoken to me three years earlier in the State of Guerrero, Mexico, was ringing loudly in my heart. "I will raise up a work in Kansas that will support you on this field." It was a Word of faith. I asked Sue to accompany me to the bus station, and it was then that I told her I was going to Kansas. A friendship had developed between us, but I still had no understanding that Sue would one day be my wife.

As we parted at the bus station, I didn't tell Sue that I only had enough money to get as far as San Pedro Sula (two hours from Tegucigalpa). San Pedro Sula was north, Kansas was north, so I would take the first step in that direction with the money I had. I bought a ticket and told her goodbye.

When I arrived in San Pedro Sula, the Spirit of the Lord told me to go to the airport. By now, I had learned that I didn't need to understand everything to obey. Going to the airport made no sense to me, but I went anyway. Arriving there, I sat down in the waiting room. I began to watch and wait to see what would happen. The airport was small and informal. I waited for some time and then noticed a cargo plane land. The pilot and another man got out of the plane and came walking through the waiting room.

Instantly, with no forethought, I greeted them and asked where they were from. They had flown from Miami, Florida. I then asked when they were going back. They told me early the next day. Out of my mouth came the words, "Mind if I ride along?"

They replied, "Sure. Be here early tomorrow morning."

I flew to Miami and began hitchhiking to Kansas. Besides my backpack and Bible, I had a treasure in my heart worth more than millions of dollars. The treasure was the Word of Faith that I had heard God audibly speak three years earlier as I stood alongside the road in Guerrero, Mexico. The Word was, "I will raise up a work in Kansas that will support you on the mission field." How would God do it? I was headed to Kansas to find out!

> Sue continues...
>
> After Duane left for Kansas, my pastor, Gloria King, was leading a women's retreat. It was a day of prayer and fasting with times of worship and personal ministry. I had been raised Mennonite all my life and, at age thirteen, had made a formal commitment to Christ and was baptized. However, as the years went by, I began to experience a personal faith crisis. As I studied the Bible, I came across scriptures like in the Gospel of John, "Most assuredly, I say to you, he who believes in Me, the works that I do he will do also; and greater works than these he will do, because I go to My Father" (John 14:12).
>
> I wasn't seeing these "greater works" in the Mennonite community, not even the regular works of Jesus: healing the sick, casting out

demons, or opening blind eyes. Could it be that the Bible was not relevant to this age? With that small opening of unbelief, I became cynical, and it soon opened doors of rebellion in my life.

When I arrived in Honduras as a missionary, Gloria recognized my inner rebellion and was waiting for the right time to minister to me. This coincided with about the time Duane left for Kansas.

At a women's retreat, I awaited my turn for personal ministry. I willingly opened my heart to her. That willingness released God's power to work through her. As the anointing came upon me, I was delivered of several spirits of rebellion that were troubling my life. I was broken before God. As I continued in weekly discipleship meetings with Gloria and the other women leaders, the Word of the Lord came to me. The Word was that I would one day be Duane Kershner's wife! God had spoken it to my heart!

Astonished, I was meditating on what I had heard when Pastor Gloria approached me with a penetrating look. I said, "Gloria, I will be married someday, and I know to whom."

She responded "And I also know who too!"

I replied, "So what do I do with that?"

She said, "Consider yourself a married woman!"

An amazing change in my life took root. Gloria continued to minister to me, and as we studied the book of Esther (how Esther had a time of preparation before being presented to the King), I knew I was in a time of preparation. It had taken Esther one year; how long would it take for me?

Three years later, I received a letter from Duane Kershner. The time had arrived! Duane, now in Kansas, had previously set apart a time of prayer and fasting. He was specifically asking the Lord to reveal to him his wife. The face and name of Susan Rohrer came to him. He hardly knew me! He had not seen me for three years! Because of the missions calling on his life, it was very important that he marry a woman with the same calling.

He did not know, nor did I, that as a baby in my mother's arms, my mother had responded to a missionary calling. Being a farmer's wife with obligations, she could not go; therefore, at the altar, with tears in her eyes and a sincere heart of faith, like Hannah of old, she dedicated me to the Lord as a missionary. Years later, after Duane and I were married and on the mission field in Mexico, my mother told me the story. She had not wanted to "make it happen." She had waited on the Lord!

I responded to Duane's choosing me. We both knew that God had sovereignly ordained our marriage, and we both said yes. We were married on March 25, 1979.

17
The Move of God in Kansas

Duane continues…

After flying to Miami in the cargo plane, I found a fellowship of believers. During their worship service, they were singing songs. "Any day now, we will all be secretly raptured and taken away." This was a strange new sound to my ears. In Mexico and Honduras, we knew nothing about books, tapes, and the vast supply of Bible teaching that existed in the USA. All we knew was the Bible and, of course, we had read about the rapture, but wasn't it when Christ returns and when every eye will *see* him?

"But in those days, after that tribulation, the sun will be darkened, and the moon will not give its light; the stars of heaven will fall, and the powers in the heavens will be shaken. Then they will *see* the Son of Man coming in the clouds with great power and glory. And *then* He will send His angels, and *gather* together His elect from the four winds from the farthest part of earth to the farthest part of heaven" (Mark 13:24–27 NKJV).

I was puzzled! One reason I had fled from the Children of God movement was that in secret, they had given me some "inside information;" they informed me that the Lord had returned! Where was he? As a baby Christian, I was shaken and found a quiet place to call out to God. It was then and there that the Holy Spirit spoke to me out of the Book of Matthew, "Therefore if they say to you, 'Look, he is in the desert! do not go out; or Look, he is in the inner rooms!' do not believe it. For as lightning comes from the east and flashes to the west, so also will the coming of the Son of Man be" (Matthew 24:26–27).

"Then the sign of the Son of Man will *appear* in heaven, and then all the tribes of the earth will mourn, and they will *see* the Son of Man coming on the clouds of heaven with power and great glory" (Matthew 24:30 NKJV).

I began hitchhiking to Kansas. Along the way, a tent evangelist gave me a ride. He was certain that I was sent from God to help him. For a couple of nights, I assisted with his meetings but then told him I couldn't stay. God was sending me to Kansas.

Oh, my poor parents! How they must have wondered what had happened to me when they saw this skinny guy with long hair, ragged clothes, carrying a guitar, a Bible, and backpack. Having sold their farm, they were now semi-retired and living in Rozel, a small Kansas town. When I arrived, I kept thinking about what happened to Lucas, my first disciple in Mexico City. When he told his parents about his encounter with Jesus Christ, they put him in a mental hospital. I stayed as low-key as possible. There was simply no way to explain all that had happened to me. I considered I could very easily experience the same fate as Lucas if they thought I had lost my mind.

Then second night at my parents' home, about 11:00 p.m., the voice of God woke me and told me to walk two blocks down the street and knock on the door of the house on the corner on the right side of the street. I got up and started to get dressed. Then I thought, *No, I can't do that. Besides, I don't know who lives there.* I climbed back into bed, and I heard it again, "Get up and walk two blocks and knock on the door of the house on the right corner."

I got up again and got partly dressed, my natural mind resisting: *Is that really you God?* I returned to bed. Again, this time, the command was stronger, "Get up!" So I did. I slipped on my worn-out shoes, grabbed my jacket, and set off down the street. It was winter, and I can still hear the crunch of snow under my feet as I walked in the dark. It was about midnight now.

I reached the house and knocked, and two young men opened the door. They were drinking and smoking marijuana. I could smell it. They just looked at me, left the door open, and walked away. I went in, closed the door, and sat down on the sofa. *Oh, God, this is terrible*, I thought. My heart was pounding. What was I doing here? In the meantime, the two guys had disappeared into another room of the house. A few minutes passed by, but it seemed like forever to me. Then another man walked into the house. I knew him. His name was Ron Bryant. He had been four years ahead of me in high school, but I remembered him. I had not seen him for ten years.

He stared at me and was shocked to see me sitting on the sofa! He said, "Is that you?"

I answered him, "Yes, it's me."

He asked, "What are you doing here?"

We were in his rental house. We began to talk. Ron got saved that night, and soon, the rest of his family received Jesus, and I baptized all of them in a nearby river. This caused no small stir. Ron was well-known in the community. He was very bold about sharing with everyone what had happened to him. Subsequently, a church started in his home. Rather than party on Saturday nights, Ron had church. Reluctantly, I became the pastor. I had no idea how to be a pastor; I had never been to church. In a limited way, I only knew about winning souls and making disciples I didn't know what a pastor really did. But God had said he would raise up a work in Kansas. Was this it?

God began to move powerfully in people's lives. They were getting born again, baptized, and filled with the Holy Spirit. It was like a holy epidemic. I was insecure about being a pastor, so I felt a need to find a place to fast and pray away from everyone. I decided to leave town and go to a town down the road where there was a hotel. When I arrived, I assured the hotel manager not to be concerned because I was going to fast and pray for ten days.

On the fourth day, I was kneeling beside the bed, praying, when I felt someone enter the room. The door was locked, but there was a definite presence in the room. Without looking up, I asked my Father God, "Who is here?"

Immediately, I heard this verse of scripture, "But the Helper, the Holy Spirit, whom the Father will send in My name, he will teach you all things and bring to your remembrance all things that I have said to you" (John 14:26).

The person of the Holy Spirit was in the room. I had been listening and obeying his voice for several years, but I hadn't known him as a person. The third person! I finished the fast and returned to my small Rozel flock. I was excited and told them I had met the third person, the person of the Holy Spirit. They didn't understand yet.

The experience of meeting the Holy Spirit was so overwhelming that I decided to go to the Colorado Mountains for two months to be alone with him. I realized I had to separate myself to get to know him better. It was summer, and Ron loaned me his old jeep. I had no idea where I was going in Colorado, only that I had to do it. I would spend the summer with the Holy Spirit, getting to know him.

He led me to a rancher near Gunnison. The rancher was moving his cattle to an upper meadow for the summer. In this meadow sat an old camping trailer that he used for elk hunting. I told him the honest truth of why I was there. The rancher stared hard at me, scratched his head, and told me to use the trailer.

It was a beautiful location and a glorious time. I spent two and a half months alone with the Holy Spirit in the upper meadow. I had taken some provisions with me, and there was a stove in the trailer and a mountain stream fifty feet away. The stream was loaded with brook trout! All I had to do was quietly crawl up to the stream, throw in a line with a hook (no bait), and instantly, I had a fish! I talked to the Holy Spirit each day, just as anyone would visit with a best friend. We walked the trails together, watched the elk, listened to the rushing mountain streams. But mostly, the Word of God was opening to me like never before.

At one point, I fasted for twenty-one days. It was during this time of fasting that I asked of God two things: Who was to be my wife? And would he give me further confirmation about my calling? He showed me that Susan Ruth Rohrer would be my wife. As for my calling, the Holy Spirit continued to impress upon my heart that I would be a church planter, and this calling included Mexico. I had not seen Susan since leaving Honduras three years before, nor had we communicated. This would have to be God! We hardly knew each other! I did not know that she was in Costa Rica, studying Spanish, and planning to become a full-time missionary. As for the calling,

I would return to Kansas and continue to walk by faith according to the word God had given me: "I will raise up a work in Kansas to support you on the missions field."

An amazing miracle of God happened. Susan and I were brought together. Later, by cassette tape, I asked her to marry me. Miraculously, the tape reached her in Central America. She answered by cassette tape, "Yes, when?" We were married six months later on March 25, 1979. We then took a six-month honeymoon to get to know one another in Mexico before beginning our pastoring together in Kansas. It all began by *faith*.

God did what he said he would do: "Raise up a work in Kansas." He took out a precious group of people for his name from among the small communities of central Kansas. He was pouring out his Holy Spirit as the Charismatic Movement was sweeping across many parts of the United States in the 1970s and 1980s. It was an exciting and fresh outpouring of his Spirit.

After the first work in Rozel, Kansas, Sue and I worked another ten years planting a church in Larned, Kansas. This was a precious wave of his glory as many people came to the saving grace of Jesus Christ. From the down and outers to the up and outers, God was saving, baptizing, and filling with his Spirit a people for his name. Sue and I grew together and also grew to love the precious flock God was giving us in Kansas.

Part Four:
Time for the
Missionary Call
to Southern
Mexico

18
Divine Alignments for Divine Assignments

Oh, the depth of the riches both of the wisdom
and knowledge of God! How unsearchable are
his judgments and his ways past finding out!
—Romans 11:33

During our years of pastoring in Kansas, a missions support base
was developing. I was conscious of what God said he would do: "I
will raise up a work in Kansas that will support you on the Mexico
mission field."

There were two other very significant things God did in preparation for our mission assignment to the unreached tribes of southern Mexico. He graced us with the ability to lead "short-term mission
teams." Year after year, through the 1980s, we planned, administered,
and took mission teams into Mexico. The work of these teams had
a great impact and helped prepare the way for our eventual move to
that field. Secondly, God gave us *strategic alignments* which have
enabled us to this day.

During the 1980s, God aligned us with Pastors Billy Joe and
Sharon Daugherty of Victory Christian Center, Tulsa, Oklahoma.
Sue and I attended their Victory Bible Institute during the winter
session of 1987. It was there one morning while in Bible class that
the Holy Spirit spoke to my heart, telling me we would take that
school to Mexico. Victory Bible Institute has proven to be a great

tool in helping us make disciples from among the indigenous nations of southern Mexico.

After the session of Bible school, we later attended missions school. Victory World Missions Training Center helped prepared us for what was ahead. Attending this school also caused us to have a deepened relationship with Pastors Billy Joe and Sharon. When the time came in 1990 for us to be "sent out," not only did our loved ones from Kansas send us, but Victory Christian Center also commissioned us. This "sending" included a team of graduates from the Victory World Missions Training Center for the work to which the Holy Spirit was calling us.

Pastor Billy Joe had encouraged us to take the entire missions class of 1990 with us to help establish the mission base. Of the twenty-five students, only three women and one young man had the calling and courage to follow us over 2,000 miles south to a place they had never been, to a people they did not know, to help us build a mission base that would bring salvation to thousands of people. In the natural, it was "mission impossible." Would we even get across the Mexican border? With God, all things are possible.

19

The Mission Base Property Revealed

It was while Sue and I led short-term teams that ministered in the crusades and outreaches during the 1980s that the Holy Spirit began to show us the need for a missions base. If we were going to sustain a movement of making disciples and planting churches, a training center would be required. We began to realize that the three following aspects would be needed to extend the kingdom of God among the tribal people: a compassionate medical ministry that would open the way into closed regions and become an evangelistic tool, a Bible school for the training of disciples taken from among the indigenous people, and a school of worship that could bring forth worship leaders and musicians trained to allow the presence of God to inhabit the praises of the indigenous converts in the local churches we would plant.

Our mission was not about imposing a traditional religion upon the people we were called to; rather, we were to introduce them to the presence of the living God. For this work, a mission base would be necessary, a center for training and outreach. Therefore, during the times we were in Mexico with short-term mission teams, we looked for property. It was in 1988 during one of these times that the Holy Spirit "did it again." He placed a word in my heart; the word was "Roca Blanca." After the other short-term team members had returned to the United States, Sue and I arranged to go look for Roca Blanca. Where was it? What was it?

We set off early one morning, packed in a pick-up truck with three young couples and their children, to search for the place. After several hours of driving, we discovered that Roca Blanca is a small island approximately three quarters of a mile off the Pacific coast, near the small fishing village of Cacalotepec. Mostly descendants from east Africa live along this coastal region. The Spaniards brought slaves to Mexico generations ago to work in the gold and silver mines. Many of these Africans had settled along the southern coast. Those living in Cacalotepec make their living diving for oysters and lobsters at Roca Blanca Island and fishing in the local lagoons. There were no boats at that time. Divers had to swim to the island.

After a while on this deserted beach in front of the island, the children were beginning to get restless and thirsty. The waves had been fun, but the sun was hot. Our purpose was completed. We had found Roca Blanca, and it was now time to go. Strangely, however, I could not leave. I told Sue that I felt constrained. If she wanted to leave with the families, she could go, but I could not. It made no sense. This was a deserted beach! As time passed, I created some real stress with our friends, not to mention Sue. The children were crying, and now everyone was really ready to go, except me. Sue agreed to stay with me because she didn't want to leave me there.

That decision created more stress. Our friends were getting upset. Finally, they piled into the pick-up truck and spun off, leaving Sue and I standing alone on the beach. The sun was setting, and Sue was trying to be a calm wife as we walked to the village of Cacalotepec. Now it was dark, and mostly, all we could see of the local people was the whites of their eyes. I believe we were the first foreigners ever to arrive in this place.

Their homes were thatched huts made of palm branches. There was one building, a small store. We bought something to drink, all the time being observed by the natives. Finally, we managed to catch a ride into the next town where there was a small "half-star" hotel. Dear Sue! We slept fitfully through the night, and at last, morning came. At the crack of dawn, I got Sue up to get back to Roca Blanca.

Once we were on the beach, I continued telling Sue I "needed" to get out to the island. It looked like a long swim for a Kansas boy.

The ocean waves were somewhat calm that day, but still, a swim to the island was a challenge. Eventually, two men came walking down the beach. They were divers planning to swim out to the rock. After some "serious" consideration, they allowed me to swim along with them. The men began to dive while I managed to get out of the waves by climbing up on the edge of some rocks, avoiding the prickly sea urchins.

The view from Roca Blanca Island looking at the Missions Base property

While perched there, I was looking at Sue way over there, sitting on the beach with the beautiful palm groves surrounded by the mountains in the background. As I glanced at a certain palm grove down the beach from where Sue was sitting, suddenly, there was a flash of light as if a flash camera had just gone off before my eyes. Then to my surprise, the Lord God audibly spoke to me and said, "That's your mission base property!"

I was astonished! In a few minutes time, everything began to come together in my understanding. That's the reason I couldn't leave the day before and why for one year I heard in my spirit, "Roca Blanca." God was positioning us! I told the fisherman "Adios," jumped in the water, and swam back to Sue. Once I got through the surf, I called out to her, "Our mission base property is just down the beach!"

We ran most of the way until we got to the property. What was this place? There stood a two-story house and another building that looked like it had possibly been a kitchen. What looked to have been a restaurant was close by. The palm roof had collapsed on both facilities. The grounds were totally overgrown; however, we pushed our way through and got to the house. We called out several times, but no one was around.

We climbed the stairs to the second floor of the house. As near as we could tell, the facility had eight rooms, each with a private bathroom. However, they were unfinished. The place was in the rough; some of the rooms did not have doors and were piled full of old lumber, bricks, etc. On the second floor, we came to a room with a door. We knocked and called out. No one! Cautiously, I opened the door. To our pleasant surprise, this room was finished and even partially furnished. The bathroom was tiled and had fixtures. I told Sue, "We will live here." We did! For ten years, we lived in that room.

After some more exploring, we joyously thanked God for the property. We prayed for the protection of the property and asked for Jesus's blood over it. Then we headed to the airport to catch our flight back to the States. How amazing are his ways!

Traveling again to southern Mexico in 1989 and after another outreach, we prayed for an angel to guide us. We then began searching for the owner of the property. We arrived at Cacalotepec, the village next to the property, and made our way down the trail leading to the palm grove over which we had prayed one year before. As we walked, a little boy joined us, and as we were approaching the palm grove, I asked him his name. He replied, "My name is Miguel Ángel!"

I said, "Miguel Ángel, early this morning, we prayed for an angel to guide us. Who is the owner of this property?"

Miguel Ángel led us to his daddy who lived in the village. Bartolo, his father, had worked for the owner. We learned that she was a widow woman living in Acapulco. Her name was Eva Luz Havana. Bartolo gave us her phone number, and we caught a bus going up the coast to Acapulco. After a small delay caused by the back axle of the bus falling off, we eventually made it to Acapulco.

Upon arrival at the home of Eva Luz, we introduced ourselves as pastors from Kansas. We explained how a year before, we had seen her property and shared our desire to develop a Bible school, music school, and a medical clinic on her land. As we shared these things, she began to cry. Between her tears, she explained that she had been waiting eight years for us! What? She began to tell us that she knew the Lord Jesus, that the palm grove was a gift to her from her mother. After her husband died, she and her nephew had attempted to build a resort on this beautiful beach front land. However, for various reasons, the project had failed, the nephew moved away, leaving her with an unfinished eight-room hotel, facilities for a kitchen, and what was to be a restaurant.

Left alone with a palm grove on her hands and an unfinished dream, one day, with a sad heart, Eva was praying and walking on the beach in front of the property. She happened to step on a figure in the sand. The figure was made of plastic and looked like a shepherd with a shepherd's staff. As she picked it up out of the sand and held it in her hands, God spoke to her heart and told her not to sell the property. He would send a pastor that would use it for his glory.

As she cried and told us this story, she was taking out of her purse the figure which she had held onto for eight years. She showed it to us and shared how she had been tempted several times to sell the property but had held it by faith, waiting for the pastor to come!

We made a first step arrangement. We rented the palm grove with a promise to clear the land and give her the money from the coconut harvest each year. The relationship began. She handed us the "pastor figure" that she had kept in her purse for all those years, and it became a "token of faith" for the trials we would face.

20
The Sending and the Arrival

How then shall they call on him in whom they
have not believed? And how shall they believe
in him of whom they have not heard? And how
shall they hear without a preacher? And how shall
they preach unless they are sent? As it is written:
"How beautiful are the feet of those who preach
the gospel of peace, and bring glad tidings of
good things!

—Romans 10:14–15

From the time that the Holy Spirit had shown us the missions base
property, two years had passed. At about 5:00 p.m. on July 5, 1990,
our caravan of young inexperienced missionaries arrived at the site.
We managed to drive through the thick undergrowth of this abandoned palm grove that would become the Roca Blanca Missions
Base. We had been driving for six days, beginning in Larned, Kansas,
where we had been sent out (blessed and released) by the local church
that Sue and I had founded and pastored for ten years. Next, we were
blessed and sent again by Pastors Billy Joe and Sharon Daugherty
from Victory Christian Center in Tulsa, Oklahoma. We were a caravan of six overloaded cars: two married couples helping with the
move, in addition to three single women, and one single man with
us. All had graduated from the missions training center at the Victory
Christian Center in Tulsa.

Sue and I were the only ones who had seen the property the Lord was calling us to develop and the only ones who had ever been to Mexico (except for our team member, Gina). It was best that no one else really knew where we were going or what we were up against. They might have backed out. None of us could have imagined the battles we were going to face.

The border crossing from the United States into Mexico turned out to be traumatic. It dragged on for two days. The officials kept sending us back across the bridge for one reason or another. They would not let us cross. We already had our legal papers, so this was not the problem. They just would not let us take our belongings. Finally, at 2:00 a.m. on the third day, the Lord prompted me that we should go now! I woke up everyone, we climbed into the packed cars, and drove across the bridge again. Unbelievably, this time, the guard was asleep. We simply drove through with no questions asked. The whole drama reminded us of an old western movie—sombrero over the guard's eyes, sound asleep in his chair, and away we went!

After arriving at the missions base, those who chose to remain with us were Linda Andrus, Nic Gathers, Laura Pratt, and Gina Gaxiola. Linda had a degree in physical therapy, Nic Gathers was a nineteen-year-old young man with the fire of God in his bones. Laura Pratt, who held a masters in nursing, would be in charge of medical missions, and Gina Gaxiola was from Mexico and had graduated from the Victory Bible and mission schools. The two couples who traveled with us on this pioneer journey had made only a short-term commitment. Therefore, the missions team would be made up of Sue and I, young Nic, and the three young women—Linda, Laura, and Gina.

It all looked a little foolish. Who were we to evangelize, disciple the nationals, and then plant churches with them? Just to clear the land and establish the necessary facilities of the base property was a million-dollar project. We had a $300 per person, per month mission support commitment from Victory Christian Center. In the natural, it was laughable that we would even survive. Along with the many challenges we would face, Sue and I did not understand that my nervous system had been damaged during the war in Vietnam by a chemical called Agent Orange. I was beginning to experience chronic pain day and night, suffering from peripheral neuropathy. We were totally dependent on the grace of the Lord Jesus Christ.

Early each morning, our team would worship, meet with the presence of the Holy Spirit, and cry out to God for wisdom, grace, and the anointing. Out of weakness, we were made strong. Gradually, the "heavenly vision" was forming in our hearts. Our commission would be to establish a beachhead, a base. From this base, we would go into the unreached tribes, evangelizing, calling, and then training and discipling an army of nationals. We would then send them back into their communities to establish local churches, churches that would house the Glory of God in the midst of the pagan idolatry, the witchcraft, and the violence that existed. "Thy Kingdom come, Thy will be done on earth as it is in heaven."

So here we were in this abandoned overgrown palm grove with its unfinished eight-room house, a kitchen with no roof, a dining area with an aged palm-thatched roof and a rotted board floor. It was gently raining when we arrived. Our travel-weary young team looked wide-eyed at Sue and me.

Eva Luz, owner of the property, had traveled from Acapulco along with her nephew, Fernando. Fernando had built the house on the property that we would live in and later buy. They came to welcome us and our team. We held hands and prayed.

21

No Small Task, the Work Begins

Now the work began. It would be no small task to clear out all the rooms of the house and finish the remaining construction work that was lacking: tiling, bathroom fixtures, doors, windows, and the list goes on. The kitchen and what would become our dining hall also needed repairs. After we had sweated and labored for days, these areas were becoming usable.

Gradually, we cleared walking trails through the underbrush. It was thick and tropical. We soon discovered we were not alone. There were snakes, scorpions, bats, and yes, mosquitoes living in the thick brush. Now we were understanding why Jesus had made the following declaration: "Behold, I give you the authority to trample on serpents and scorpions, and over all the power of the enemy, and nothing shall by any means hurt you" (Luke 10:19). It was all becoming very real, and numerous times since, we have taken authority after a scorpion bite; in the name of Jesus, the pain and poison is stopped. In the beginning, there were deadly coral snakes in the underbrush. The Word is real. We have the power and authority in Jesus's name. Nothing has harmed us.

We were not unnoticed. Oh no, we were being watched. We knew, no doubt, that we were the talk of the Cacalotepec community. We worked out an arrangement with them, and for a daily wage, our neighbors from the village came to help us, equipped with machetes, to hew out this wild jungle growth. These people were acclimated to the tropical heat that plagued us. We quickly made friends, and a much-needed interdependence developed among us. It worked like this: We had some funds which they needed, and they had the strength and acclimatization which we needed.

It seems every village, town, or city has soccer teams in Mexico. Our neighboring village of Cacalotepec was not an exception. We had a panel truck during those early days. It was named the "Ark!" We would haul the local soccer team to their games, and Sue would sit on the top of the "Ark," filming the games. This brought us great favor was another "link" into the local community. We were gaining their confidence, and gradually, some were accepting the living Jesus, and their lives were being transformed. Therefore, the first church plant was with our neighbors, and today, a lively church of around 200 people shines in our local village.

During the 1980s, when we were making short-term trips to Mexico, we had particularly worked with the Mixteco Indians and the coastal peoples in the state of Oaxaca. Churches had sprung up as a result, and now members of these churches came to our aid. Teams of youth and men from the churches would bring their machetes, strength, and knowledge, helping us clear the land. Others teams of believers also arrived to help us. Many came from churches in the United States. These dear brothers and sisters in Christ were some we had come to know and love since the early 1980s.

On one occasion, a group of Mixteco Indian youth were at the base, helping us. In this group was a young man by the name of Ismael. His parents had both died, and he came from a very poor Mixteco village. Ismael was planning his wedding. He and our young team member, Nic, from Tulsa, Oklahoma, had befriended one another as they labored in the hot sun with machetes, clearing the land. Ismael had persuaded me to officiate the wedding, but now he also needed transportation for the wedding party. In those days, there was very little public transportation, and three-ton cattle trucks were commonly used to haul people. Nic, moved with compassion and wanting to help Ismael, made an arrangement.

A man who owned a three-ton truck was buying our coconuts. He would haul the coconuts across the mountains where he could sell them at a good price, then on the return trip, he would load his truck with vegetables from the Oaxaca Central Valley. On occasion, we would trade coconuts for vegetables. Now we needed a truck. Therefore, Nic made an arrangement, trading his Ford Bronco for the three-ton truck to use over the weekend to transport the wedding party. The date arrived, and off we went on the three-hour drive to the Mixteco Indian county where the wedding would be held. Sue and I drove a van to transport the bride and her family while Nic would bring the family of the groom in the truck.

The truck was packed, as well as the van, but we all safely arrived at the site of the wedding. All went well. We performed the wedding ceremony and were seated at the banqueting table. The band was beginning to play, and the food was being served when suddenly, the Holy Spirit spoke to me. He firmly told me to return to the mission base. I told him, "But I can't just leave now!"

He was firm with me. I had to go. I turned to Sue and told her I had to leave. By now, she had gotten somewhat accustomed to this kind of thing, but still, it was somewhat of a stretch.

I left Sue with the van and tried to excuse myself gracefully from the festivities. Now I would have to get to the highway and find a ride back to the base. It was challenging, but I arrived at the base just before dark. Waiting at the gate of the base was one of our new converts. He was very troubled and proceeded to tell me that the man who had Nic's Ford Bronco had shot and killed his wife and the body had been left in Nic's vehicle! The police would be waiting for Nic when he arrived with the three-ton truck. *Oh, no!* We prayed, then took one of the base vehicles and drove several miles down the highway to stop Nic and Sue as they were returning.

Another team member drove the truck back to the base. Nic was taken to the nearby town of Puerto Escondido where he could get a lawyer. The lawyer advised Nic to leave the country until things cleared up. In those days, to fall into the hands of the judicial police could be very difficult. They could ask for a large sum of money and leave Nic in jail until they got it.

The Holy Spirt had warned us. In the process of time, it all worked out. The man who killed his wife was jailed, Nic returned, recovered his vehicle, married, and planted a church.

22
Time to Begin Building

By late1990, the cleanup work was advancing as well as the out-reaches. The time to build had arrived: cleanup, outreaches, building, and discipling—this would be our lifestyle for years! A medical clinic facility would be needed from which we could give care and stage the Compassionate Medical outreach. Bible school facilities were needed: classrooms and also dorms to house the disciples who would come from the indigenous tribes. The kitchen and dining hall had been repaired and were now adequate for starters. The music school would also need classrooms where instruction and training of worship leaders would take place.

The churches would need well-trained leaders. Therefore, in 1991, we broke ground by faith and began building the first dormitory for the Bible school. It is important for the reader to understand that each step was by faith since we still did not formally own the property! We were planted on the land legally, but we did not own it. I simply knew it was ours by "the Word of Faith" I had received that memorable day when I swam to the rock and God audibly spoke to me, "That palm grove is your missions base property!" I could never forget that.

Because we were not Mexican citizens, the law stated that we could not own beachfront property. This law could be our reason to fail. However, we knew without a doubt that God had a plan. At each step, we would ask, "How will God lead us through this one?"

This is how he did it. In 1993, we formed a nonprofit Mexican corporation, The Victory International Cultural Center, Inc., and another miracle happened. The corporation was approved by the Mexican Federal Government with me, Duane Kershner, as the president and Susan Kershner as the vice president. We were now officers in a legal entity with full rights to buy property. Our donors answered with financial provision, and the same year, we purchased the first portion of land from Eva Luz. On this land, we would build the main facilities of the base. The first purchase is a story in itself. Since then, we have continued to fight the good fight of faith, purchasing land and building facilities.

The missions base today contains the following training schools and ministries:

1. Victory Bible Institute—a three-year discipleship training program.
2. School of music—a three-year program to train worship leaders and musicians.
3. K–12 bilingual Accelerated Christian Education school.
4. A state-accredited high school for indigenous students.
5. A Spanish-language school for missionaries and Christian workers called to Latin America.
6. The Corban Medical Clinic.
7. The New Day Children's Home.
8. Roca Blanca Guesthouse for short-term teams and visitors.
9. Fountain of Grace Healing and Deliverance Center.
10. Events Ministry: Annual Family Camp Meeting ("Convocation") where approximately 5,000 people are in attendance for three days of revival the week of Easter; Church Camps; Children's Summer Camp; Church Conferences; Marriage Enrichment Retreats.
11. The headquarters for the network of churches affiliated with Roca Blanca.

The Roca Blanca Mission Base is legally registered with the Mexican Government, Secretary of Religious Affairs.

Roca Blanca Missions Base 2020

23
The Training Center in Operation

Bible School Classroom and Girl's Dorm

By September of 1993, we had finished building the first two-story dormitory as well as the men's bathrooms for the Bible training center. We had repaired the kitchen and equipped it, plus the dining hall was now usable. The main house was far enough along that we could use all the rooms. We began the first year of Victory Bible Institute, using the second floor of the men's dormitory as a classroom with the male students living on the first floor. The female students lived in rooms in the main house, sleeping in three-tiered bunks. We started with eighteen students who were from the indigenous Chatino and Mixteco tribes along with certain disciples we had called from among the coastal towns. Linda Andrus was the director of the school. Today, over 1,200 disciples have graduated since that early beginning.

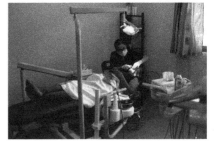

Medical Clinic and Staff

Our nurse, Laura Pratt, had been treating people and holding medical clinics since our arrival. We used the dining hall as a make-shift clinic, hanging bedsheets as room dividers with cardboard boxes full of medicine and medical supplies. Hundreds of people were coming for help. The first visiting short-term medical team arrived from the United States in 1991. The word got out, and over 1,500 people swarmed the base, crying out for medical help. At the time, there were no doctors or clinics in many of the towns and villages. Thanks to the many doctors and medical teams that have come from the United States during the past twenty-five years, today the Corban Medical Clinic, built on the base, shines as a beacon of compassionate medical help and a center from which medical outreaches are staged. Over 125,000 people have received free medical care in the villages and at the base clinic.

Missions Base in Operation

Music School

In 1988, God gave me a vision of a school to train musicians and worship leaders. We would need sanctified and prepared musicians for the churches we would plant. But who would be the director? Charles Norton, from Goshen, Indiana, came on a visit to the base in 1993. He had a degree in music from Western Michigan University. He caught the vision! The dream of a school of worship was about to begin. Charles joined the missionary team and began to develop the program. Since its inception, the music school named "School of Worship and Prophetic Music" has trained hundreds of worship leaders and musicians for the local churches.

After several years of development, Charles turned the school over to Sergio Cruz. Sergio, a musician from Mexico City, came to the Bible school at Roca Blanca in 1996. He finished and became director of the mission's base worship team. Later, he took the directorship of the music school. Sergio and his team have trained hundreds of musicians who are now serving in the churches.

Please take a few moments and consider this: Praise and worship had never ascended to God from these tribal people who are hidden away in the rugged Sierra Madre Mountains. There were none who had been redeemed by the blood of the Lamb! Never in their history had the "Song of the Lamb" been heard from these hearts. Never had the vapors of praise and worship ascended to heaven from these people. They have had forms of religion, mixtures of idolatry and witchcraft. But songs of praise to the living God had not been heard, especially in their native tongue.

Today, in these mountains, the "songs of the redeemed" are being sung by a redeemed people who are offering thanksgiving and praise to him who alone is worthy. The Word, Jesus Christ, is on their lips and in their hearts.

> But the hour is coming, and now is, when the true worshipers will worship the Father in spirit and truth; for the Father is seeking such to worship him. (John 4:23)

24

The Church Planting Movement Begins

I will build My church, and the gates of Hades
shall not prevail against it.

—Matthew 16:18

The mission of the Roca Blanca Mission Base is church planting: live churches filled with the Word of God and the Holy presence of Jesus Christ in every unreached village and city. Thus, the training center at the missions base must train and equip disciples of Jesus Christ who can establish and lead churches. Fast forward from 1990 until today. There is now an established network of sixty-seven indigenous churches in eight geographic and language districts. These churches are pastored and led by disciples who have graduated from the Roca Blanca Training Center.

There are seventeen tribes of indigenous people in the state of Oaxaca. During the past twenty-nine years, the Roca Blanca Missions Base has worked planting churches with the following tribes: Amuzgos, Chatino Alto, Chatino Bajo, Mixteco Alto, Mixteco Bajo, and the Zapotecas. We have also planted churches with the coastal populations from Pochutla to Pinotepa National and in the capital city of Oaxaca.

Following is an example of a church plant among the Chatino Indians who were formerly classified as an unreached people group.

It was during a time of prayer and fasting in 1991 that God gave me a vision of his Holy Spirit being poured out upon the Chatino Indian tribal people. They live high up in the Sierra Madre Mountains, north of the mission base. In 1990, they were officially classified as one of the "unreached people groups," or in other words, there was no witness or personal knowledge of Jesus Christ among them. To the contrary, in this mountainous region of the Chatino Indians, there is a "high place."

In the City of Juquila, legend is that generations ago, "the virgin" appeared there. Just as in the Book of Acts where the "goddess Diana" was worshipped in Athens, so now the virgin of Juquila is also worshipped. Juquila is a well-known idolatry center throughout Mexico.

Thousands of Chatino Indians living in the mountains around Juquila were trapped in this deception and the witchcraft that goes with it. In truth, the virgin of Juquila is a plastic idol dressed as a woman and placed in an elaborate shrine. People travel for hundreds of miles to give money, worship her, and ask for special favors. It is a very lucrative business supporting hotels, restaurants, buses, taxis, and the sale of all kinds of idolatrous trinkets and artworks. One advantage of this idolatry is the highway built to reach Juquila from Oaxaca City. In 1990, travel into the Chatino villages and towns surrounding Juquila required four-wheel-drive vehicles, especially during the rainy season. We were thankful for the logging trails that had been opened by companies who were harvesting the pine trees. Now, God had given the vision, but how would we go into this unreached region with the commission of taking out a people for his name? There would be great opposition.

The roads we traveled

We understood that with the calling comes the protection if we do it correctly. Jesus said, "First, bind the strong man, then take his goods." The strong man would be the principality over Juquila, his goods being the lost souls of the Chatino people. "Let the high praises of God be in their mouth, And a two-edged sword in their hand" (Psalms 149:6).

As Psalms 149 instructs, at the missions base, we began warfare in praise combined with fasting and prayer, waiting for the door into the Chatino region to open. Then it happened! One Sunday, Sue and I traveled to the mountain village of Santa Cruz to minister at a Sunday service.

Santa Cruz is located in the lower mountains on a dirt road leading into the Chatino district. When we arrived, a man from Panixtlahuaca, which is a Chatino town of around 10,000 people, was waiting for us. His name was Raymundo García. An evangelist by the name of Juventino had traveled into Panixtlahuaca and had led Raymundo to the Lord. However, Juventino had left the area because of death threats on his life. Before leaving Panixtlahuaca, Juventino passed on to Raymundo a cassette recording with me preaching about the Baptism of the Holy Spirit. Somehow, Raymundo learned that we were going to be in Santa Cruz and came with an intense hunger for the baptism of the Holy Spirit.

He walked the long distance and waited three days for our arrival. When we arrived, we found Raymundo eagerly waiting for us. When we prayed for Raymundo, he received a powerful baptism of the Holy Spirit. Returning to Panixtlahuaca with the power of the Holy Spirit, he led around twenty people to the Lord. A few weeks later, Raymundo made the long journey to the mission base and pleaded with us to come to his town. The door had opened! We were to bring medicine as some of the people were very sick. There was no doctor or government clinic in the town at that time, only witch doctors.

After praying and fasting, we felt peace to go. The base nurse, Laura, a young intern, and I would take medicine in a four-wheel drive Jeep. We drove for ten hours to where Raymundo was waiting for us. He traveled with us the last three hours and directed us to his house. We were the first people from the United States to ever visit this very isolated and closed indigenous town. There was no public transportation and only one vehicle in the town. That vehicle was owned by the city.

A crowd of around forty people was waiting for us in front of Raymundo's house when we arrived. We stepped out of the Jeep onto the rocky street, and with Raymundo translating into the Chatino language, we shared the basic Gospel message. Several people received the Lord Jesus at that time. What a glorious welcome! We unloaded the medical supplies and immediately went to work caring for the people. Early the next morning, the local authorities showed up to inform Raymundo that we were not welcome and needed to leave town. The atmosphere became tense. We loaded the supplies, told our host goodbye and turned the key to start the Jeep. It would not start!

What were we to do? Should we walk out, leaving the jeep and the medicines? After prayer and discussion, it was determined that I would go for a mechanic. Raymundo walked to the edge of town with me, and I began the long walk up the dirt road that led to Juquila.

The locals could make the walk in three hours, cutting through the pine trees on their familiar trails, but I didn't know this area. God, in his great mercy, helped me. Soon after I began walking, I met a truck, and the driver assured me that he would make his delivery and then take me to Juquila where I could catch a bus.

When I arrived in Juquila, there was no bus, but I caught another ride in the back of a truck, and finally, around midnight, arrived at Roca Blanca. I set out in another vehicle to find Sergio, a local mechanic. Sergio had helped us with some vehicle repairs before. Although somewhat reluctant, he agreed to make the long difficult trip to Panixtlahuaca. We arrived late the following afternoon, and Sergio went to work.

Meanwhile, Laura was still caring for people, and they kept coming. Raymundo was tense; the city authorities had been to see him again. They were being pressured by the Catholic priest, and we were being told to leave. It was now night, and I can still remember our mechanic, Sergio, being very frustrated. Throwing his ball cap on the ground, he told me he couldn't find anything wrong. He didn't know what had happened with the Jeep. After a while, he entered the house which was full of Chatino Indians.

Raymundo insisted that I preach, but I was exhausted. He stood by me to translate from Spanish to Chatino as I tried to share a few things. I began with no real anointing, trying to tell them about Jesus and his imminent return.

Then I stopped, and the Holy Spirit whispered to me, "Tell them about the Holy Spirit." So I did.

Immediately, the atmosphere changed. Suddenly, like the day of Pentecost, the Holy Spirit fell in the room. People began to scream and fall down. They were speaking in tongues of the Spirit and crying. They were seeing visions of Jesus in the room and even began to prophesy. They had never heard of prophecy! Tim, the intern, worked his way through the Holy commotion and pointed out to me that the mechanic was praying in tongues. How could that be? He wasn't even a believer! Now he was! All of this continued until around 1:00 in the morning when the people began to leave. We were witnessing the birth of a church in this place!

Early the next morning, we knew we had to leave, so we decided to pull the Jeep with the other vehicle which Sergio and I had driven. While Tim and Sergio were trying to tie the rope to the other vehicle, I sat down in the Jeep and turned the key: *The Jeep started!* What? It turned over just as if there was nothing wrong with it. Our sovereign God had held us there until the Holy Spirit was poured out; the Chatinos had experienced the supernatural power of God, and the mechanic was saved and filled! A church was birthed. Today, there are approximately 1,000 members in the Panixtlahuaca church. Three other churches have started out of this work, and at the time of this writing, the believers at Panixtlahuaca are building an auditorium for 1,500 people.

There are many other testimonies that could be shared about this work. For the first three years after the work began, the persecution was very intense. However, many were coming to know Jesus, and the church outgrew Raymundo's home. One weekend, I went to Panixtlahuaca and drew up plans for the church facility. Land had been given, and we knew the building would be a big step and cause a reaction, but it was time. The work could not increase anymore in Raymundo's home.

After drawing the plans and making arrangements, construction workers from the missions base traveled the twelve-hour trek to Panixtlahuaca to begin the construction. Early the morning that the work began, men in a nearby wooded area began firing on the construction workers. The first believer, Juventino, the man who had evangelized Raymundo, was shot five times—three bullets in the chest, one in the stomach, and one in his leg. He died! But twelve hours later, God sent him back! It was a totally undeniable miracle. Juventino lived another twenty years. In 1997, Benny Hinn ministries filmed this miraculous story and televised it worldwide: Glory to God!

The Panixtlahuaca story is only one church plant history. Each church plant has its own story. The birthing of a church is like a child being born into a family, each one distinctly different, yet of the same bloodline: the blood of Jesus in this case.

The Panixtlahuaca Church celebration, January
2020, on their new property site

Baptisms of the Chatino Indians

Below is pictured a map of Oaxaca, each star showing the location of a church that is part of the Roca Blanca network of churches. They are color-coded to show the tribe and dialect.

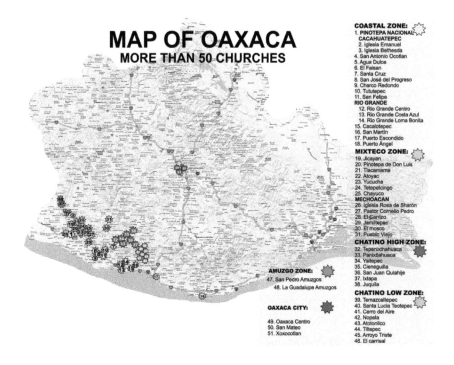

MAP OF OAXACA
MORE THAN 50 CHURCHES

COASTAL ZONE:
1. PINOTEPA NACIONAL CACAHUATEPEC
2. Iglesia Emanuel
3. Iglesia Bethesda
4. San Antonio Ocotlan
5. Agua Dulce
6. El Faisan
7. Santa Cruz
8. San José del Progreso
9. Charco Redondo
10. Tututepec
11. San Felipe
RIO GRANDE
12. Rio Grande Centro
13. Rio Grande Costa Azul
14. Rio Grande Loma Bonita
15. Cacalotepec
16. San Martin
17. Puerto Escondido
18. Puerto Ángel
MIXTECO ZONE:
19. Jicayan
20. Pinotepa de Don Luis
21. Tlacamama
22. Atoyac
23. Yucucha
24. Tetepelcingo
25. Chayuco
MECHOACAN
26. Iglesia Rosa de Sharón
27. Pastor Cornelio Pedro
28. El Carrizo
29. Jamiltepec
30. El mosco
31. Pueblo Viejo
CHATINO HIGH ZONE:
32. Tepenixtlahuaca
33. Panixtlahuaca
34. Yaitepec
35. Cieneguilla
36. San Juan Quiahije
37. Ixtapa
38. Juquila
CHATINO LOW ZONE:
39. Temazcaltepec
40. Santa Lucia Teotepec
41. Cerro del Aire
42. Nopala
43. Atotonilco
44. Tiltepec
45. Arroyo Triste
46. El carrisal

AMUZGO ZONE:
47. San Pedro Amuzgos
48. La Guadalupe Amuzgos

OAXACA CITY:
49. Oaxaca Centro
50. San Mateo
51. Xoxocotlan

117

25
Understanding Our Assignment

Below is a map of the State of Oaxaca, Mexico,
showing the ethnic distribution.

Ethnic Distribution

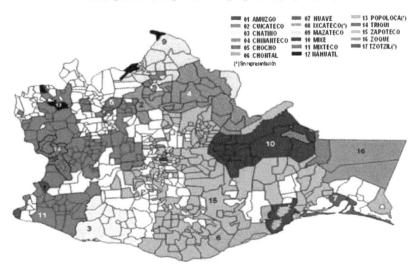

01 AMUZGO	07 HUAVE	13 POPOLOCA(')
02 CUICATECO	08 IXCATECO(')	14 TRIQUI
03 CHATINO	09 MAZATECO	15 ZAPOTECO
04 CHINANTECO	10 MIXE	16 ZOQUE
05 CHOCHO	11 MIXTECO	17 TZOTZIL(')
06 CHONTAL	12 NÁHUATL	

(') Sin representación

When we arrived here in 1990, the State of Oaxaca, Mexico, was classified as containing the greatest concentration of unreached people groups in the entire Western Hemisphere. There are seventeen tribes of indigenous people living in the rugged mountains of Oaxaca. They speak 155 dialects. *We are here to take out a people for his name from among these tribal people. That is our assignment!*

In Acts 15:14, "Simon has declared how God at the first visited the Gentiles to take out a people for his name." Even as Peter was first sent to the Gentiles at the house of Cornelius in Acts chapter 10, so God sent us to Oaxaca to take out a people for his name. What a great honor, and this honor is shared by all who have helped and partnered with us over the past thirty years. As the Apostle John was writing the book of Revelations, he got a glimpse beyond the veil; he saw the redeemed. "[F]or You (Jesus) were slain, and have redeemed us to God by Your blood Out of every tribe and tongue and people and nation" (Rev. 5:9). There will be a redeemed people from every tribe and tongue and people and nation.

In 1971, when God first sent me walking down the southern coast of Mexico, he began to open my eyes and my heart to these people. Then he sent me to Kansas for fifteen years to build a support base and make alignments for the assignment. There with my wife, Sue, he was maturing us and developing the necessary relationships to launch the mission. With God, all things are possible, yet how would we ever penetrate into these closed pockets of isolated people? When we arrived in 1990, there were very few roads leading into the indigenous villages and towns. In some places, there was still no electricity. Many of the people did not speak Spanish but spoke only their native dialect. They lived in adobe homes and cooked on dirt floors.

Gradually, God revealed his divine strategies. Our team was directed to fast, pray, and ask for the tribal people: "Ask of Me, and I will give You The nations for Your inheritance, And the ends of the earth for Your possession" (Psalms 2:8).

We were to do warfare in praise, binding the ancient principalities that held these people groups captive. As it is written, "Let the high praises of God be in their mouth, And a two-edged sword in their hand… To bind their kings (principalities) with chains"(Psalms 149:6,8).

After prayer and spiritual warfare, we were to wait for the doors to open. We would then go in with compassionate medical care and demonstrate the love of God to the people, showing that we truly cared for them. Then we could share in spirit and in truth the living Christ. Once the people of an indigenous community began to receive Christ, we would select the disciples from that community and dialect, bring them to the missions base, and disciple them. We were not to religiously indoctrinate them but rather work with the power of the Holy Spirit and the Word of God, allowing a true transformation to happen.

Once the process of maturing was further along, we could send the disciples back to their communities, work with them, and establish the local church in each community.

First Bible School Class 1994

Graduating Classes 2019

Moving forward to the time of this writing, today there are approximately 8,000 established believers in the native churches. With every church plant, there has been persecution. Even as I am writing, we have reports of five new believers who have been jailed in a Chatino Indian town where the Gospel was recently preached. This, of course, is not new to the Gospel. Peter and John were jailed when "in the name of Jesus of Nazareth, a lame man was healed" (Acts 4). In the early days, there were death threats toward us, just as there was severe persecution toward many of the early disciples. Quite often, the new believers are jailed for not participating in the pagan festivals. New believers are threatened and at times driven off their land and out of their communities if they do not renounce the Gospel.

We are very grateful for the many medical teams from the United States that are helping us fulfill our assignment, giving of their time, skills, and finances. Villages have opened to the Gospel and churches have been planted because of this joint effort. The Roca Blanca team working with short-term teams from the USA causes an acceleration in the outreaches.

Medical Missions and the Roads

As early as 1993, we began to realize that we would need a guesthouse for visiting teams. Short-term teams are a sacred part of the assignment; the plan of God. The Great Commission is given to every believer: "Go into all the world and preach the Gospel" (Mark 16:15). With the architectural skills the Lord has given and with the help of generous donors who "caught the vision," plus a diligent crew of construction workers, today the Roca Blanca Base offers a beautiful air-conditioned nine-bedroom guesthouse for visiting teams. The guesthouse has an ocean view from each room and offers excellent food services on the fourth-floor dining area.

Roca Blanca Missions Base Guesthouse.

View of Roca Blanca Island from Guesthouse

Fountain of Grace Ministry of Healing and Deliverance

There has come an intensified call upon us in the areas of healing and deliverance. Therefore, in 2017, we began to formally develop what we call "The Fountain of Grace," which is a healing and deliverance ministry at the Roca Blanca Missions Base. People have traveled from the United States and from different parts of Mexico to stay at the guesthouse while receiving healing and ministry. One of the greatest healing miracles that occurred at Roca Blanca in 2019 was the Lord Jesus Christ healing my wife, Sue, from stage four aggressive breast cancer. The cancer had spread from her left breast and was in her lungs. The CAT scan revealed "innumerable nodules" throughout her lungs.

Three weeks after the confirmed diagnosis, Sue received the prayer of faith with the laying on of hands (James 5:14–15). The Holy Fire of God filled her lungs at that time, and she was healed. When we returned to the hospital, where she was to receive numerous treatments of chemotherapy, the doctor could not find the lump in her breast. Later, the PET Scan showed only four small nodules in her lungs. We were led by the wisdom of God to do follow-up alternative cancer treatment at the Oasis of Hope Cancer Treatment Hospital in Tijuana, Mexico. In the month of October 2019, Sue received her last PET scan and blood test in Tulsa, Oklahoma. All her reports show she is completely cancer-*free*.

At the time of this writing, over 3,500 people have received ministry at "The Roca Blanca Fountain of Grace Ministry." This is a fresh call of God upon our lives. The second- and third-year students of the discipleship school along with us on the ministry team are in a new time of training led by the Holy Spirit. As the darkness increases on the earth, much more shall his glory be seen through the preaching and demonstration of the "Gospel of the kingdom."

> And this Gospel of the kingdom will be preached
> in all the world as a witness to all the nations, and
> then shall the end come. (Matt. 24:14)

Jesus teaches us about the signs of the end-time in Matthew 24:4–15. Among these signs, one of the most important is the sign of the Gospel of the kingdom being preached: "And this Gospel of the kingdom will be preached in all the world as a witness to all nations, and then the end will come" (Matt. 24:14). When Jesus spoke of this, he was prophesying about something that would happen during the end times. The preaching of the Gospel of the kingdom is not just the Gospel of salvation. It is the end-time declaration of his kingdom confirmed with signs and wonders. Thus, in God's great mercy, he is giving all nations the opportunity to fully decide who they will follow: Antichrist or the living true Christ. Therefore, at this time in history, there is a call of the Holy Spirit for all who will hear, obey, and prepare. The call is to make ready for the "double portion anointing... And he will cause the former rain and the latter rain (double portion) to come down for you" (Joel 2:23). This double portion anointing is the enablement to declare the Gospel of the kingdom with power and signs following. This will bring in the greatest world harvest ever, just before the Lord's return.

The Lord is waiting for the precious fruit of the earth until he has received the early and the latter rain (James 5:7). In the book of Acts, we see the early rain, the first outpouring of the Holy Spirit. We see the results of that outpouring. In Acts 8, for example, when Philip went down to the city of Samaria, he preached the kingdom of God with power. People were saved, healed, and delivered: "And many who were paralyzed and lame were healed" (Acts 8:7). This was the fruit of the early rain. The prophet Joel has prophesied there will be a double portion anointing during the latter rain for those who have prepared and consecrated their lives.

In the book of Matthew 25:1–13, Jesus teaches the parable of the wise and foolish virgins. The "five wise virgins" had made preparation. They woke up, trimmed their lamps, and set their lives in alignment with the final move of the Holy Spirit before the Bridegroom came.

The Holy Spirit is calling for a return to the original discipleship commission, the original apostolic call: "And when he had called his twelve disciples, he gave them power over unclean spirits, to cast them out, and to heal all kinds of disease" (Matt. 10:1). This calling is an important aspect of the Roca Blanca assignment.

26
Confrontations

Religious Resistance

I will now return to our story and some of the early confrontations we faced after arriving at the missions base property in 1990. With all of this activity, it did not take long for the news to spread that a group of foreign missionaries had arrived and were clearing the beachfront property near Cacalotepec. We were progressing in the work, getting along with the local people, and forging on with the vision. But soon, we received a bit of a surprise.

One morning, a "welcoming" procession of around 200 people walked onto the property. The procession was led by several Catholic nuns. The two priests who were with them waited outside the gate. The nuns explained to us that the local people were uneducated, and it wouldn't be a good idea to give Bibles to the people. "Why?" I asked.

"Because they would not be able to understand since some could even possibly lose their minds if they began to read the Bible."

It couldn't have been more evident that this group was not happy about our presence! We went back to work. A few weeks passed, and sure enough, they returned. This time, they acted more aggressively and made it very clear that we were not welcome. After some very oppressive comments, they walked away. However, an amazing thing happened to them. As they walked down the road, they passed by some very large trees. In these trees, there were wild bees. As the procession walked by these trees, the bees came down. They began to sting and chase the people. The group broke into a run, screaming and waving their arms to get away from the bees. They never came back.

> And I will send hornets before thee, which shall drive out the Hivite, the Canaanite, and the Hittite from before thee. (Exodus 23:28)

Nevertheless, some days later, the local priest showed up. He kindly invited me to a meeting with him the following Saturday morning. He suggested we meet next to the village of Cacalotepec. This was to be a friendly visit between him and me. That seemed good on the surface, but what was really happening? We spent time in prayer over this situation.

Saturday morning soon arrived. This time, two priests arrived with an angry mob they had organized. They indirectly held me captive throughout that day. They conducted an informal trial, and I was the accused. The official director of the county was with them, seated at a formal table with the two priests. The priests took turns making accusations against me to stir up "their" crowd. The day had been well-planned; the people even brought food and drinks.

At one point, they demanded my legal papers. I presented copies which were never returned. The day dragged on. Finally, around 4:00 in the afternoon, a lady from our neighboring town who was quite drunk called everybody to attention. Waving her arms, she declared, "Let the *greengos* (gringos) live over there. We will live over here, and everybody will be happy!" The people began to laugh, and the crowd gradually dispersed.

Later, the death threats began. Word was sent to us that if we didn't leave, some would die. Sue and I took the team and left for Puerto Escondido, which is a tourist town around twenty miles away. We rented rooms in a hotel and began to pray. After two days, all of us arrived at the same position of faith. We had to stand our ground. This mission was God's plan. He was directing us. After all, God had said, "This is your mission base property." We loaded up again and returned to the base. Several years later, we were invited by a family to their home for a special barbecue. They had recently accepted Jesus Christ as their savior and were feeling God's correction or conviction. They had been part of the group that was asked to get rid of us. They sincerely asked our forgiveness.

Here Come the Bandidos

To those around us, it appeared that we had money. We had a four-wheel-drive Jeep and a couple of four-wheel Suburbans that our precious people in Kansas had provided to help us get through the rugged mountain logging trails leading to the Indian populations. Therefore, in the early days, we were confronted time after time with bandidos. These bandits would come late at night, armed and masked, knocking down our doors and carrying away all they could manage. These invasions were not the only danger. Hostage-taking in Mexico was becoming a popular, profitable business. Our area was not exempt.

Late one night, after we had been robbed, the armed masked men gathered us all together and they called me out. My heart began to leap in my chest; I was being taken. In those days, people in our area who owned land and cattle or businesses were being taken hostage and held for ransom. Their families were forced to pay $30,000 to $50,000 dollars to get their loved ones back. Some were being killed. Perhaps one could find a way to escape, but usually, selling land or raising money in whatever way they could to pay off these crafty and violent bandits was the only option. Now it was me in this precarious position as twelve well-armed masked men were escorting me off the property.

Just two weeks before, our small faithful group of missionaries had met to pray about this impending threat. The locals had been warning us. We decided there was no way other than to trust God. We made a decision before God in prayer that in Jesus's name, we simply would not be taken. Now the test had come!

I was praying in the Spirit silently as I was being walked to the beach gate that leads off the property. We were only a few feet away from the gate when I stopped abruptly. The anointing of God came on me, and with a loud voice, I proclaimed, "In the name of Jesus Christ of Nazareth, I am not going!"

The men froze! I turned and began walking back to the house. One of them began to follow me, walking about three feet behind me with a shotgun pointed at my back. I tried to ignore him and kept on walking. As I approached the house, my faithful wife came running down the stairs. While we were being robbed, she had kept a $50 bill hidden away. As I reached the house, she handed the $50 to the man with the shotgun. He bolted, and they all began to run. It was totally supernatural.

The Colombian Drug Lords

Some weeks later, early one morning, I was on the rooftop of the house, praying; the sun just coming up. That big yellow ball was rising again out of the beautiful blue waters of the Pacific Ocean, the scene declaring the glory of God to me when I saw something unusual. A twin-engine boat came racing ashore almost in front of the missions base. Two men jumped out of the boat, doused it with gasoline, and torched it. The blaze was intense as the fiberglass boat began to burn. The men ran! This was not a normal fishing experience!

I then began to observe something else; our neighborhood fishermen who had spent the night out in their boats began to move about. They were picking up some containers that were floating in the water. The containers were full of cocaine! I had witnessed a Colombian drug drop! The fishermen began to haul their "catch" home with them!

I believe most of our local fishermen were somewhat innocent (or ignorant) when they took the containers home to their thatched huts and dirt floor dwellings. But not for long! And now, what were they going to do with all these bags of "white powder?" Looking at a map of this hemisphere, you will discover that Colombia is straight south of the lower Mexico coastline where our mission base is located. Drugs are transported from Colombia by boat or by small aircraft and then dropped in the ocean at certain prearranged locations. Local fishermen, contracted to recover the product, then turn it over to the next member of the drug delivery supply chain. However, in this incident, something had gone wrong. Was the boat that carried out the drop being followed?

Two days later, our somewhat sleepy village of Cacalotepec was not quiet. Drug lords arrived in Suburbans with darkened windows, and all hell broke loose. They held me for two or three hours for questioning, claiming that the big guys in Colombia had my name. In the village, they went house to house, beating up men, women, and children in search of the drugs. Some of our neighbors quickly gave back the product, but others had run away, taking the goods with them, endangering us all. The drug dealers were intense to get their product back.

Our team began to intercede in prayer. Fortunately, no one was killed, and the storm passed. We have learned the importance of keeping our ocean and community free from drug-trafficking through prayer and intercession.

> For he shall give his angels charge over you, to
> keep you in all your ways. (Psalms 91:11)

This was the beginning of the challenges we would face. In every trial God was faithful to deliver us. There have been hurricanes, earthquakes, and floods, including the intense spiritual battles we have faced confronting ancient forms of witchcraft and voodoo.

Earthquakes and Voodoo

Along the southern coast of Mexico are settlements of descendants from East Africa. These descendants were brought to Mexico by the Spaniards generations ago to work in the gold and silver mines. Today, many of them are fishermen while some also work in the coconut grooves that blanket the southern coastline of Mexico. There has been no major evangelistic thrust to date among these people. However, our movement has penetrated some of the small villages that are close to the mission base.

It was from one of these villages that we received a young Afro-Mexican student in the Bible school in 1997. We were very pleased that he was with us; however, we knew very little about him. A young pastor who was opening a work in one of the Afro settlements had brought Juan to us (name changed).

After only three weeks with us, early one morning, I heard terrible screams coming from the men's dormitory area. I ran quickly to see what was happening. I found Juan lying in the grass, dressed only in his underwear and covered with blood. He had gone into the kitchen where other students were making the early morning coffee. Juan had taken a butcher knife and began stabbing himself. I was telling some of the workers to run for our nurse, Laura, when suddenly, Juan jumped up and began to run away. Some of the young men climbed into one of the base pick-ups and went after him. He ran all the way into our neighboring village of Cacalotepec.

The young men had to forcefully tie him down with ropes and bring him back to the base. Juan had become demon-possessed. We did not know that his father was a voodoo priest.

We placed him in our medical clinic where he was washed and calmed. I asked two of the young dormitory pastors to stay with him. Around 9:00 a.m. the same morning, we experienced a 7.4-magnitude earthquake! It seemed like the quake lasted forever. When things stopped shaking and the dust settled, we were thankful that only one person on the missions base had been injured and most of the existing facilities had held up. However, we were just building the school of music; the walls lacked the top header, and $50,000 worth of walls had fallen down. We gathered everyone for prayer and were assessing what to do when one of the dormitory pastors came running from the medical clinic. He told me that Juan had plucked out his eyes and that his eyes were lying on the floor of the clinic. For a few moments, my mind blacked out! We were in intense spiritual warfare.

The entire State of Oaxaca was declared a disaster zone because of the earthquake. Bridges were out, roads were closed, thousands had been injured and many killed.

The months that followed were extremely difficult. We were accused of surgically removing Juan's eyes, saying that we had sold them. We were also accused of trafficking organs. This, of course, brought us under intense investigation. The voodoo priest stirred up horrible accusations against us. We were brokenhearted for Juan; he had lost his eyes. However, through it all, we watched the salvation of the Lord: The captain of the judicial police was Christian. He understood. The Attorney General was a Christian; he understood. After intense spiritual warfare, the case was closed.

> In all of this we are more than conquerors through
> him who loved us. (Romans 8:37)

27
Future Vision

This story is not over. The making of disciples and church-planting continues. The second generation, our sons and daughters in the faith, have received their batons and are running in the race. This race will not end until Jesus appears in the clouds with great power and glory.

From the Roca Blanca Missions Base in the State of Oaxaca, we are lifting our eyes and looking toward the State of Guerrero, which borders Oaxaca on the north. In the State of Guerrero, many Afro-Mexicans live along the coast. They are basically unreached with the Gospel of Jesus Christ. In the interior of Guerrero are the Aztec Indians who are hidden away in the mountains and still unreached. The famous tourist city of Acapulco is located on the coast of Guerrero where the drug lords are fighting for control. The entrance into Guerrero (which means warrior), will be the greatest spiritual warfare battle in the history of our ministry. Some may even lose their lives.

Generations ago, the Spaniards brought slaves from east Africa to Mexico, using them as a source of labor to exploit the gold and silver from Mexico. Many of these Africans, now Afro-Mexicans, eventually settled along the southern coast of Mexico in the states of Guerrero and Oaxaca. They are fishermen by trade or work in the vast coconut groves that blanket the coastline.

Unfortunately, there has never been a major missionary work among these people. Spiritually, many continue their ancient practices of voodoo, spiritism, and varied forms of witchcraft. The Aztecs who live in the interior of the state in the Sierra Madre mountains have a mixture of religion, combining Catholicism and the ancient pagan practice of worship to the winged serpent god, Quetzalcoatl. Adding to this "mix" are the drug cartels that have settled in Acapulco. These drug "lords" are becoming another spiritual force. Many are using the demonic spiritual forces of the "Santa Muerta Cult" (Holy Death Cult). These drug lords war for dominion, taking control of entire cities and killing all opposition. This is warfare for spiritual control in ignorance of the real ruler and eternal King Jesus Christ.

> And Jesus came and spoke to them, saying, "All authority has been given to Me in heaven and on earth. Go therefore and make disciples of all the nations, baptizing them in the name of the Father and of the Son and of the Holy Spirit." (Matt. 28:18–19)

In 1971, I was supernaturally sent to the Aztec Indians in the state of Guerrero. It was there that I first heard the audible voice of God: "I will raise up a work in Kansas to support you on this mission field." That has happened. The Holy Spirit led us to begin in the State of Oaxaca, which borders Guerrero on the south. For thirty years, we have been raising up an army in preparation to move into Guerrero. Previous pastors and missionaries have left the interior of Guerrero in fear of the drug lords.

After we advance and gain territory in Guerrero, the next missionary phase in the history of the Roca Blanca Mission Base will be sending missionaries to other parts of the world. Oaxaca is the poorest state in Mexico but rich in human resources! These rugged, humble people from Oaxaca (some looking like they are from the Middle East) will become missionaries. Think about that! Roca Blanca will be a training and a sending base to the nations. This story is just beginning!

Sue adds:

> For forty years, I have been at Duane's side. It has not always been easy. However, God has enabled me to yield to the Holy Spirit throughout this

journey. Jesus has been faithful to give "his faith" to me, enabling me to walk confidently in the Word and will of our Father God. Numerous times, we have gotten out of the boat and "walked on the water" by faith, Jesus calling, "Come!"

After twelve years together in Kansas, planting two local churches, and at last having our own home, a steady income, and even a second rental home, we left it all to follow the call, "Come!" We moved to the Mexico mission field, giving away the two homes, our pastor salaries, our precious flock, and started over in an abandoned coconut palm grove when Duane was forty-five, and I was forty-two years old.

Called to build a missions base and penetrate into the unreached indigenous tribes of southern Mexico, we both have been held at gunpoint numerous times. By the powerful name of Jesus, Duane escaped from being taken hostage for ransom. It has been a journey. Perhaps in God's wisdom, Duane and I have no biological children of our own. Instead, he gave us the privilege of giving birth to hundreds of spiritual children, God's family, to whom we have opened our hearts and lives. The "Word of Faith" that Duane and I received that we would become husband and wife has been a strong foundation for our marriage. "And this is the victory that has overcome the world, our faith" (1 John 5:4).

As any couple, we have had our challenges, the calling on our lives causing lots of spiritual warfare. Literally thousands of people have come to the saving grace of Jesus Christ in southern Mexico because we answered "The Call." Jesus died for them 2,000 years ago, but a price must be paid to fulfill his last great command. "All authority has been given to me in both heaven and earth, therefore, Go ye into all the world…" We are so humbled and honored to have been chosen.

People of Oaxaca

Private Elementary School at Roca Blanca

Roca Blanca High School

Spanish School Roca Blanca Language Training
for Latin American Missionaries

"New Day" Children's Home Roca Blanca

Annual Camp Meeting at Roca Blanca

Faithful God
Pastors Duane and Susan Kershner on the Roca Blanca Mission Base

To Learn More About Roca Blanca:
www.rocablanca.org
(https://www.youtube.com/watch?v=g17Zy1bVYZI)

The Roca Blanca Stateside Office:

Roca Blanca Missions
2228 Dover Drive
Hutchinson, KS. 67502
Phone: 1-918-688-0117

E-mail: rocablancamissions@gmail.com

About the Author

Duane Kershner and his wife, Susan, have been full-time missionaries living and working with the indigenous tribes of southern Mexico for the past thirty years. They are the founders of the Roca Blanca Missions Base located on the coast of Oaxaca, Mexico. The Roca Blanca Base is a model for world missions and indigenous church plant movements. There are seventeen indigenous tribes living in Oaxaca that speak 155 distinct dialects. In 1990, the state of Oaxaca was classified as having the greatest concentration of unreached people groups in the Western Hemisphere.

Today the Roca Blanca Base has graduated over 1,000 disciples from among the tribal people. These disciples pastor and lead, at the time of this writing, a network of sixty-six indigenous churches. Co-laboring with the Holy Spirit, the Roca Blanca Missions team continues to take out "a people for his name."

CPSIA information can be obtained
at www.ICGtesting.com
Printed in the USA
BVHW052233290521
608404BV00002B/6